I0124054

The Aftermath of a Global Pandemic

The Aftermath of a Global Pandemic

Authors

Austin Mardon
Ameer Hasan
Dollyann Santhos
Maggie Wang
Jason Zhou
Ryan Baxter
Amal Rizvi
Ivy Truong
Megan Ng
Paige Breedon
Christina Nguyen
Kazma Faheem
Jaelyn Kupilik

Edited By

Joy Xu

Copyright © 2023 by Austin Mardon

All rights reserved. This book or any portion thereof may not be reproduced or used in any manner whatsoever without the express written permission of the publisher except for the use of brief quotations in a book review or scholarly journal.

First Printing: 2023

Typeset and Cover Design by Josh Harnack

ISBN: 978-1-77369-892-2
eBook ISBN: 978-1-77369-893-9

Golden Meteorite Press
103 11919 82 St NW
Edmonton, AB T5B 2W3
www.goldenmeteoritepress.com

Table of Contents

Introduction

Pandemics are loosely defined as a disease or condition that persists on a large magnitude, typically on a country, continent, or world basis. Though these incidents are not an everyday occurence, its once-in-a-lifetime existence can provide insightful recognition of humanity's social structures and potential gaps. Part of these elements can be derived by observing the resonance of its effects after the peak of pandemics. Thus, it is vital to approach global pandemics through multifaceted perspectives.

Chapter 1
Unanswered questions: the Plague of Justinian and parallels to the medieval Black Death

By Christina Nguyen

During Justinian's reign in 541 AD, there was an epidemic that posed a threat to human civilization as a whole. The plague has been traced from Britain to Syria, encompassing the entire planet and ruining civilization at the time. The bacterium that caused the Black Death in the fourteenth century has since been discovered on human bones from Justinian's reign, suggesting that the historian Procopius may have some accurate observation of the Justinian epidemic. The extent of its true devastation remains an open topic. This essay explores how we currently understand this ailment and the difficulties we encounter when learning more.

The era

The longest-reigning and most prosperous Roman emperor of the sixth century AD, Justinian was born into a relatively low-class family. He was born in a Roman world that is centered on the city of Constantinople (now called Istanbul), after the last Western empire's ruler had been overthrown by barbarians. He was a very successful Roman emperor, living in a Greek-speaking world with barbarians to the West and Persians to the East, and he was a Christian in a world where there were very few remaining pagans. He was a magnificent military conqueror and the creator of the Hagia Sophia. Unfortunately, Justinian was also emperor when this plague first appeared in the Mediterranean region.

The plague occurs

People began getting sick in significant numbers in the 540s. The principal signs, as mentioned by the historian Procopius and others, were a severe and abrupt fever, buboes, and other minor symptoms (swellings on the body) ("Procopius on the Plague of Justinian: Text & Commentary - World History Encyclopedia" n.d.). However, different individuals displayed other varying symptoms, and frequently the symptoms appeared to be at odds with one another: some individuals were comatose while others remained conscious, others had pains in head, neck and throat, others were vomiting and had the bloody flux; and some individuals passed away right away while others did so after enduring a prolonged period of suffering. The general populace was gripped by a sense of panic and anxiety ("Procopius on the Plague of Justinian: Text & Commentary - World History Encyclopedia" n.d.).

With a population of over 500,000, Constantinople was a sizable city; ominously, it was claimed that this epidemic was attacking about 15,000 people daily. These significant numbers are mentioned by Procopius, who claims that the initial outbreak lasted for nearly four months. The initial death toll ranged from 5,000 to 10,000 each day, or even higher ("Procopius on the Plague of Justinian: Text & Commentary - World History Encyclopedia" n.d.). According to John of Ephesus, there were 300,000 total fatalities, or roughly half of Constantinople's population, or 12,000 every day. These are all beautiful round numbers, so they are not the most accurate or precise observations, but they do depict immensity.

Procopius and his observations

Procopius, a young man who later became the personal secretary to Belisarius, the important general who oversaw Justinian's campaigns of reconquest in the 530s and 540s, arrived in Constantinople. Therefore, it appears that Procopius was in Constantinople during this epidemic in 542. He is without a doubt an eyewitness to some of the incidents he recounts, and there is no reason to question how strongly the magnitude of the outbreak affected him. He wrote about it twice, once in a book about Justinian's wars where he describes the campaigns he witnessed and once in A Secret History, likely after he had retired to a life of seclusion. It should be emphasized that he was extremely harsh and scathing of Justinian and his consort, Theodora, in this second letter. Thus, that latter text has a clear ideological orientation. His earlier, more thorough description contains a wealth of details concerning the signs and human cost of the illness ("The Plague of Justinian - Diaspora Travel Greece" n.d.). The quantity of sickness and fatalities that Procopius attributes to the plague is really the source of our problems (and we will discuss this later).

Since Justinian's empire was a Christian empire, Procopius writes about this plague as an act of wrath, a wrath coming from the Christian God. Because the Jews had rejected the chosen Messiah as being Jesus Christ, the Byzantine Romans (the Christian Romans) believed that they were the true inheritors of God's promises to the chosen people ("Procopius on the Plague of Justinian: Text & Commentary - World History Encyclopedia" n.d.). The title of "the chosen people" was passed down from the Jews to the Romans as a result of this. Of course, whenever the chosen people commit sins, they naturally can expect to be punished by God for straying from the path of righteousness. Thus, the accounts that we have which ascribed the cause to the plague, or really any other disasters, referred to heretical members of the population.

Geographic spread

Even though it is very challenging for historians to piece together the story at this point from the fragmented materials they/we have, the virus clearly swept throughout Constantinople very quickly. Procopius claimed that the illness first formed in Egypt, close to Port Said/Bur Saaid (today called the Suez Canal). From the disease's heart, we can see that it expands in two directions: one to Gaza and Palestine, and the other to Alexandria and the west. From Procopius's perspective, there is an Egyptian beginning point, but when we examine other sources, we see that that is only a portion of the narrative ("The Plague of Justinian: The First Recorded Global

Pandemic" n.d.; "Procopius on the Plague of Justinian: Text & Commentary - World History Encyclopedia" n.d.). Additionally, it is claimed to have originated in northern Sudan and Africa, or even even further south (what is today called Yemen). Some 300 years prior to that, a body with what appears to be evidence of the bacteria was discovered in Kyrgyzstan. From the current understanding, perhaps it was a plague that originates in central Asia, spreads over oceanic trade lines, and finally arrives in Egypt, where Procopius first notices it. Naturally, we can trace it more effectively from there ("The Justinianic Plague | Origins" n.d.; "The Plague of Justinian: The First Recorded Global Pandemic" n.d.).

We are aware that yersinia pestis is largely an animal illness rather than a human disease ("Plague: Types, History, Causes & Prevention" n.d.). There is a vector that can enable the fleas (that reside on the animals) to jump to humans, and it spreads when an animal population that contains yersinia pestis expands and falls ("Ecology and Transmission | Plague | CDC" n.d.). That is the main route by which human populations are infected. We can make some very educated assumptions about how it travels and how the various strains infected human populations by looking at the geographical and climatic context in which those rodents lived and then relating that historically to the local human populations. The black rat and the black rat flea are believed to be a key vector for spreading the disease, though there are still questions about how it travels precisely (some of which have yet to be resolved). However, once the disease has developed into a serious condition, that does not necessarily mean that they are the primary vector of transmission.

In fact, historians are increasingly giving the transmission greater thought. For instance, it is now pretty obvious that the Great Plague of London in 1665–1666 was predominantly disseminated by human lice and human fleas, even though the original infection may have been caused by rat fleas. It is conceivable that it was one of the Black Death's vectors as well, but the problem is that there are not any specific sources for the Justinian Plague that specifically mention rats, so we do not know where to go for evidence next.

Justinian's reaction to the plague

Justinian dealt with the plague in the same way that he dealt with many other things – through delegation. He gives a worker, Theodorus, a great sum of money to solve the problem (i.e. really to find out ways to bury the masses of dead people.) Theodorus sets about managing mass burials, and to begin with, he went across the Golden Horn and poured bodies into the old towers of the fortifications on the other side. When this died over, in about four months, Justinian wrapped up all notion of plague in his nation rapidly. It went on to infect the Persians and the barbarians, of course, but that was beyond Constantinople ("The Justinianic Plague | Origins" n.d.).

The treating of the plague

In the ancient world, the concept of disease and its treatment was severely underdeveloped. A plague was defined as something that biologically kills a lot of people quickly; no particular illnesses or signs were mentioned. Of course, there were certain unique difficulties in providing extensive therapy even with the fantastic logistics systems of ancient Rome. Doctors struggled with the idea of the plague as a whole (Dattwyler 2007) therefore Procopius spoke about distinguished physicians who tried traditional treatment techniques like taking more baths and making lifestyle changes. Procopius observed that this was not particularly effective. The plague quickly spread throughout Constantinople, sparing few of the wealthy and well-off (Justinian himself fell victim to the plague). Procopius gave us the impression that the disease affected all facets of society before deviating from the expected patterns (Dattwyler 2007).

Our understanding of the Justinian plague

From our vantage point, the Black Plague that follows exhibits many characteristics in common with the Justinian Plague. The DNA of the medieval Black Plague and the Justinian Plague have been found to be genetically identical. Since we now have a firm grasp on the deadly disease (which has a high fatality rate of about 50%), we can make more parallel observations. DNA evidence has been recovered from burials in the 540s in Western Europe, where we do see Yersinia pestis.

The medieval Black Plague

A comparable pandemic decimated the population of Western Europe more than fifty years later. Between 1347 and 1352 CE, a disease pandemic known as the Black Death ravaged medieval Europe, killing an estimated 25–30 million people. It is interesting to note that the illness started in central Asia and was brought to the Crimea by Mongol troops and traders, just like historians hypothesized about the Justinian plague. Rats then introduced the plague into Europe via Italy on Genoese commercial ships

The illness was brought on by fleas on rats and was brought on by the bacillus bacteria Yersinia pestis. The Black Death was so named because it may cause sores and skin to become black, in addition to other symptoms including fever and joint discomfort. Europeans lacked the necessary preparation to face the terrible reality of the Black Death. In both men and women, according to the Italian poet Giovanni Boccaccio, there were many pus-filled swellings, either on the [groin] or under the armpits, very large in size, almost like an apple or an egg shape and size. These odd swellings, which we now call buboes, leaked blood and pus, which was subsequently followed by a number of other unpleasant symptoms, including fever, chills, vomiting, diarrhea, and excruciating aches and pains, before death quickly occurred.

The lymphatic system is attacked by the bubonic plague, which enlarges the lymph nodes. The infection may spread to the blood or lungs if left untreated. The Black Death spread horrifyingly and without discrimination: according to Boccaccio, "the mere touching of the clothing looked to itself to impart the disease to the toucher." Additionally, the sickness was horrifyingly effective. Even those who went to bed feeling fine the previous night could pass away by dawn. Scientists now know that a bacillus called Yersinia pestis spreads the plague, also known as the Black Death. (This germ was identified at the end of the 19th century by the French biologist Alexandre Yersin.) This horrific series of events is frightening but understandable today. But by the middle of the 14th century, it didn't seem to have any logical justification.

Nobody was aware of how the Black Death was spread from one patient to another or how to stop or cure it. For instance, one medical professional asserts that "instantaneous death occurs when the airborne spirit departing from the sick man's eyes strikes the healthy person standing nearby and looking at the sick". Medieval medical professionals were just somewhat more pragmatic than their Byzantine counterparts during the Justinian Plague. The medieval medical profession relied on rudimentary and outdated procedures like bloodletting and boil-lancing (practices that were unsafe as well as unhygienic), as well as superstitious customs like burning aromatic herbs and taking vinegar or rosewater baths. Healthy folks, meanwhile, made every effort to keep away from the sick in a state of terror. Priests refused to provide final rites, doctors turned away all patients, and business owners shuttered their doors. Many people escaped the city for the countryside, but even there they were unable to escape the sickness because it also affected pigs, chickens, lambs, cows, and goats, in addition to humans .

They are aware that the bacillus spreads from person to person via the air, flea and rat bites, and other means as well. In medieval Europe, both of these pests were virtually always present, but they were especially common onboard ships of all kinds, which is how the deadly epidemic spread from one European port city to the next. The Black Death quickly spread from Messina to the ports of Tunis in North Africa . After that, it arrived in Rome and Florence, two cities at the hub of a complex network of trade lines. The Black Death had devastated Paris, Bordeaux, Lyon, and London by the middle of 1348.

According to estimates, between 30% and 50% of the inhabitants of the areas afflicted by the Black Death perished from the disease, with up to two-thirds of those who contracted it passing away. The death toll was so enormous that it had a considerable impact on medieval civilization in Europe as a whole, leading to demands for the abolition of serfdom, broad rebellions, and the complete abandonment of many towns and villages due to a lack of farmers. The Black Death was the greatest disease in recorded human history, and it would take 200 years for Europe's population to return to its pre-Black Death levels.

Before the Black Death struck, the 14th century CE in Europe had already shown to be somewhat of a tragedy. Due to an earlier epidemic that had affected cattle and crop failures brought on by overuse of the land, there were two significant famines that affected all of Europe in 1316 and 1317 CE. Warfare also caused volatility, particularly the Hundred Years War between England and France from 1337 until 1453 CE. The unusually temperate cycle of 1000–1300 CE was giving way to the start of a "little ice age," in which winters got steadily colder and longer, shortening the growing season and, as a result, the harvest. Even the weather was getting worse. In addition to being helpless in terms of treatment, medieval doctors were constrained by the appalling state of sanitation in comparison to modern standards, which prevented them from doing what they could most likely have done to help people: prevent illness. Quarantining areas would have been another useful tactic, but because people rushed away in fear whenever a case of the plague appeared, they unknowingly (as they did not understand about the transmission of illnesses) carried the disease with them and spread it even further; the rats took care of the rest.

Like with Justinian, there were so many plague victims and bodies that the authorities were at a loss for what to do with them. Carts heaped high with corpses became a frequent sight throughout Europe. The only option seemed to be to remain in place, stay away from others, and pray. By 1352 CE, the disease had finally run its course, but it would recur throughout the rest of the medieval era, albeit in less severe outbreaks ("Two of History's Deadliest Plagues Were Linked, With Implications for Another Outbreak" n.d.).

The Black Death affected certain regions much more severely than others, despite its unchecked spread. It is quite challenging to estimate the total death toll because of this fact and the sometimes overstated death tolls of medieval (and some modern) authors. Sometimes entire cities, like Milan, are able to avoid major repercussions, but other cities, like Florence, are devastated, losing 50,000 of its 85,000 residents (Boccaccio claimed the impossible figure of 100,000). At its height, Paris was claimed to have buried 800 people every day, but the slaughter went unnoticed in other cities. Although some historians prefer a number closer to 50%, the average death rate in affected areas was 30%, and this was likely the case in the worst-hit cities. Thus, estimates of the death toll in Europe between 1347 and 1352 CE range from 25 to 30 million. Europe would not reach pre-1347 CE levels of population until somewhere around 1550 CE ("Black Death - World History Encyclopedia" n.d.; "Black Death - Causes, Symptoms & Impact - HISTORY" n.d.).

There would still be difficulties to overcome on a daily basis even after the crisis eased. Because there wasn't enough labor to meet demand, wages and costs rose. An important hurdle would be the necessity for agriculture to produce food for people, as well as the dramatic drop in demand for manufactured goods because there would be a lot fewer people to use them. Because individuals who could work, particularly in agriculture, were in a position to demand remuneration, the institution of serfdom, in which a laborer paid rent and respect to a landlord and never moved on, was doomed ("Effects of the Black Death on Europe - World History Encyclopedia" n.d.). Women had greater rights to own land. A more adaptive and capitalistic (every man for himself) workforce was produced. The aristocracy's attempts to rebuff these new demands led to civil unrest and frequently open uprisings. There were notable riots in Paris in 1358, Florence in 1378, and London in 1381. The old feudal structure was no longer in place, and the peasants certainly didn't get all they desired ("Effects of the Black

Death on Europe - World History Encyclopedia" n.d.). A plea for lower taxes also failed miserably.

After the terrible famines of 1358 and 1359 CE and the sporadic, albeit milder, outbreaks of the plague in 1362-3, 1369, 1374, and 1390 CE, most people's everyday lives had begun to improve by the end of the 1300s CE. The general well-being and wealth of the peasantry increased as competition for land and resources dropped as a result of a lower population. Even landowners from the aristocracy were quick to claim the unclaimed lands of the deceased, and upwardly mobile peasants might consider enlarging their holdings("Effects of the Black Death on Europe - World History Encyclopedia" n.d.)..

Some property rights that women had not previously enjoyed were granted to them, in particular. In some parts of England, for example, widows were permitted to keep their deceased husband's property until they remarried; in other, more lenient jurisdictions, if they did remarry, they were not required to forfeit their late husband's property as had previously been the case. The laws varied depending on the region. Although none of these social changes can be directly attributed to the Black Death itself—in fact, some were already under way even before the plague arrived—the shock wave it caused in European society was unquestionably a contributing and accelerating factor("Effects of the Black Death on Europe - World History Encyclopedia" n.d.).

Further correlations

Although the Justinian epidemic had an impact that was unmistakably comparable to that of the Black Death, its exact kind has long been unclear to researchers. However, in a ground-breaking new study, a group of German researchers used careful examination of skeletons discovered in a German cemetery dating back to the sixth century to recreate the genome of the bacterium that caused the Justinian plague. They discovered that Yersinia pestis (Y. pestis), the same bacteria that caused the Black Death, was the organism that caused those 50 million deaths in the Byzantine Empire ("Scientists Reveal

Cause of One of the Most Devastating Pandemics in Human History – Daily News" n.d.).The two skeletons that were used in the new study, which was written about in the journal Molecular Biology and Evolution, were taken out of Altenerding, a plague burial site in southern Germany close to Munich, fifty years ago. The sample of Y. pestis that was used to reconstruct the pathogen's genome was extracted by the researchers using a single tooth from one of the skeletons—that of a woman between the ages of 25 and 30("Microbe Behind Black Death Also Caused Devastating Plague 800 Years Earlier - HISTORY" n.d.).

The skeleton in question, according to one of the paper's co-authors, Michaela Harbeck, was discovered only a few kilometers away from the bones examined in an earlier study by a team led by Dave Wagner, a microbial geneticist at Northern Arizona University. Based on examination of the molars of two German plague victims who perished about 1,500 years ago, Wagner's research connected Y. pestis to both the Justinian epidemic and the Black Death. This connection was corroborated by Harbeck and her coworkers, but they came to the conclusion that the Black Death was not directly related to the earlier plague and was instead brought on by a genetically distinct strain of Y. pestis ("Microbe Behind Black Death Also Caused Devastating Plague 800 Years Earlier - HISTORY" n.d.; "Scientists Reveal Cause of One of the Most Devastating Pandemics in Human History – Daily News" n.d.).

The Justinian plague's genome was entirely reconstructed for the new study, and it included 30 newly discovered mutations and structural rearrangements that happened as DNA cells split apart and replicated themselves. Information from their reconstruction also pointed to the specific Y. More genetic diversity than previously believed was present in the pestis strain that caused the previous plague. The researchers are hoping that their research will provide light on the evolution, adaptation, and effects of plague, which has been a problem for mankind for almost 5,000 years and is still a problem in some parts of the world today. In recent years, outbreaks have been reported in Madagascar, Peru, and the Democratic

Republic of the Congo. The World Health Organization reports that there were 320 cases of plague reported globally in 2015, including 77 fatalities ("Plague" n.d.).

References

"Black Death - Causes, Symptoms & Impact - HISTORY." n.d. Accessed November 10, 2022. https://www.history.com/topics/middle-ages/black-death.

"Black Death - World History Encyclopedia." n.d. Accessed November 10, 2022. https://www.worldhistory.org/Black_Death/. Dattwyler, Raymond J. 2007. Justinian's Flea: Plague, Empire, and the Birth of Europe By William Rosen. 367 Pp. New England Journal of Medicine. http://www.nejm.org/doi/abs/10.1056/NEJMbkrev58338.

"Ecology and Transmission | Plague | CDC." n.d. Accessed November 10, 2022. https://www.cdc.gov/plague/transmission/index.html.

"Effects of the Black Death on Europe - World History Encyclopedia." n.d. Accessed November 10, 2022. https://www.worldhistory.org/article/1543/effects-of-the-black-death-on-europe/.

"Microbe Behind Black Death Also Caused Devastating Plague 800 Years Earlier - HISTORY." n.d. Accessed November 10, 2022. https://www.history.com/news/microbe-behind-black-death-also-caused-devastating-plague-800-years-earlier.

"Plague." n.d. Accessed November 10, 2022. https://www.who.int/health-topics/plague#tab=tab_1.

"Plague: Types, History, Causes & Prevention." n.d. Accessed November 10, 2022. https://my.clevelandclinic.org/health/diseases/17782-plague.

"Procopius on the Plague of Justinian: Text & Commentary - World History Encyclopedia." n.d. Accessed November 10, 2022. https://www.worldhistory.org/article/1536/procopius-on-the-plague-of-justinian-text--comment/.

"Scientists Reveal Cause of One of the Most Devastating Pandemics in Human History – Daily News." n.d. Accessed November 10, 2022. https://dailynews.mcmaster.ca/articles/scientists-reveal-cause-of-one-of-the-most-devastating-pandemics-in-human-history/.

"The Justinianic Plague | Origins." n.d. Accessed November 10, 2022. https://origins.osu.edu/connecting-history/covid-justinianic-plague-lessons?language_content_entity=en.

"The Plague of Justinian - Diaspora Travel Greece." n.d. Accessed November 10, 2022. https://diasporatravelgreece.com/the-plague-of-justinian/.

"The Plague of Justinian: The First Recorded Global Pandemic." n.d. Accessed November 10, 2022. https://www.thecollector.com/plague-of-justinian-byzantine-empire/.

"Two of History's Deadliest Plagues Were Linked, With Implications for Another Outbreak." n.d. Accessed November 10, 2022. https://www.nationalgeographic.com/animals/article/140129-justinian-plague-black-death-bacteria-bubonic-pandemic.

Chapter 2
Sociocultural Implications of the COVID-19 Pandemic

By Maggie Wang

Introduction

The emergence of SARS-CoV-2 and the subsequent COVID-19 pandemic has served as a major global challenge, presenting unprecedented difficulties in the realm of public health and resulting in devastating losses for many. As of lately, the public eye has been largely concentrated on the transition of the virus from variant to variant, and the impact that the pandemic has had on human health, the economy, the political sphere, and society as a whole. This chapter will take a deeper look into the sociocultural implications of the COVID-19 pandemic alongside groups of interest that have been disproportionately impacted.

SARS-CoV-2 (severe acute respiratory syndrome-coronavirus-2) is a virus that causes COVID-19 (coronavirus disease 2019), an infectious respiratory disease (Baloch et al., 2020). The contagion originally surfaced in Wuhan, China in the latter part of 2019 and has since traveled globally until it was declared a public health emergency by the World Health Organization (WHO) (Muralidar et al., 2020). Since the initial outbreak and subsequent outbreaks in global epicenters, public health measures have been implemented to curb the spread of the virus and protect against widespread infection. A notable measure includes physical distancing, where individuals were encouraged to maintain a 6-foot distance from others outside of their household, and capacity limits were enforced to reduce crowding in public areas. Despite the name entailing physical distance, a large majority of society has suitably replaced this term with social distancing, which has connotations of social isolation rather than just physical disconnectedness (Mansouri,

2020). Unfortunately, those with lower socioeconomic status and other marginalized communities lack the basic infrastructure and capacities to practice physical distancing. As a result, it is integral to examine these groups who experience entrenched social inequalities that the pandemic has exacerbated.

The Rise of Xenophobia

From the start of the COVID-19 pandemic, anti-Asian racism has been magnified within society, exacerbated by the rise of xenophobia. During various crises, whether these be healthcare related or even economic, the literature has shown that there is a pattern of scapegoating minority groups (Mansouri, 2020). Thus, these demographics often grapple with exclusionary and discriminatory behaviours and practices that are sustained by society as a whole as well as the media. The COVID-19 pandemic is an unequivocal demonstration of this principle: racism such as physical attacks, online bullying, xenophobic conspiracy theories, and more, have been perpetuated by the average citizen and even politicians. Mike Pompeo, the former US secretary of state, has vocalized these dangerous behaviors, publicly terming COVID-19 the "Chinese Virus" on more than one occasion (Wassler & Talarico, 2021). In addition, Donald Trump, the former president of the US, has blamed China for not only failing to curb the spread of the virus but also for a lack of transparency when dealing with these matters (Wassler & Talarico, 2021). These actions alone, have resulted in continual blame being placed on China and scapegoating of those that are of Asian descent. On a micro level, there have been incidents of violence against Chinese and other East Asian individuals. For example, a student from Hong Kong was refused service due to xenophobic predispositions, and a man from Singapore was violently attacked in London (Wassler & Talarico, 2021). East Asian restaurants have closed as a result of a lack of patronage and Chinatowns in various areas are deserted (Wassler & Talarico, 2021). These hostile attitudes are particularly concerning, as they indicate the capability of an unpredictable and external event to completely shift social dynamics and almost immediately heighten long-standing and deep-rooted discrimination (Mansouri, 2020).

COVID-19 as a Misinfodemic

Beyond implications for systemic racism and xenophobia, the COVID-19 pandemic has also been termed a "misinfodemic" as misinformation has been circulating rampantly through various forms (Banerjee & Meena, 2021). Over recent years, social media has held an increasingly pervasive hold on society, penetrating deeply into everyday life. In fact, over three billion individuals are regular users of social media, alluding to how significant of an impact it has on the widespread provision of information - despite whether the information is true or false (Banerjee & Meena, 2021). This aspect of social media is potentially a differentiating factor of COVID-19 as a misinfodemic as compared to past pandemics. Outbreaks of SARS, MERS, and influenza have been a huge cause of global concern; however, the media coverage and digital consumption of COVID-19-related news have been exponentially greater than these prior epidemics (Banerjee & Meena, 2021). As a result, fear-mongering, mass blame, circulating misinformation, and more, have run rampant in the media during recent years.

This widespread misinformation includes the circulation of conspiracy theories about the origins of SARS-CoV-2 alongside homemade remedies that claim to "prevent or cure the disease". For instance, theories about using garlic or incorporating magico-religious practices to cure COVID-19 have spread to all parts of the world via social media. These sources often falsely claim that the information is based on sources such as the Centers for Disease Control and Prevention (CDC) to improve their credibility with the general public (Banerjee & Meena, 2021). Alongside this, studies have also found that circulating misinformation has also contributed to mass xenophobia. For example, Hu et al. found that there was increased use of search terms "Chinese virus" or "Wuhan pneumonia" rather than the proper terminology on Google (2020).

The misinfodemic has also highlighted the concept of information overload, which can significantly impact public perceptions of health and overall mental health. Through evaluating health-risk perception theory, the fact that COVID-19 is a novel coronavirus and there was a lot of ambiguity surrounding symptoms, prognosis, and possible cures, contributed to anxiety and oversharing of misinformation (Banerjee & Meena, 2021). In addition, this uncertainty prompted a large proportion of the general public to grasp onto straws when sources regarding potential cures or preventative strategies arose in the news. As a result, this led to the stocking of fake treatments and the hoarding of medications and personal protective equipment (PPE) (Banerjee & Meena, 2021). A particular instance of this that was circulating in the media was the appearance of the antimalarial medication, hydroxychloroquine, in the news as a drug against COVID-19. Despite there existing limited evidence supporting its use for treatment against SARS-CoV-2, many people began hoarding these medications and using them regardless of their intended purposes. This unfortunately led to cardiotoxicity and fatalities in these individuals (Banerjee & Meena, 2021).

Given the profound effect of the COVID-19 pandemic on circulating misinformation, this has increased the need to scrutinize health information to identify credible and reliable information. Although social media has the capacity to spark this form of misinfodemic, it also has the potential to spread awareness regarding public health measures and education. Moving forward, the WHO has indicated the necessity of implementing a more comprehensive and thorough education program regarding public health emergencies (Banerjee & Meena, 2021). As the pandemic has highlighted many issues that arise with a lack of health literacy among the general public, this program will likely target the spread of fake news and the breakdown of complex health information into digestible formats through a collaboration between healthcare experts and the media.

The Shadow Pandemic

The COVID-19 pandemic has also illuminated the existence of the shadow pandemic, where domestic violence rates have skyrocketed behind closed doors during lockdowns. In a 2021 report by the United Nations, they evaluated domestic violence cases in Africa, Asia, South America, Eastern Europe, and the Balkans (Mineo, 2022). They found that during the pandemic, levels of violence against women have increased to concerning levels. In fact, the American Journal of Emergency Medicine found a 25-33% global increase in domestic violence cases (Mineo, 2022). Alongside this, the National Domestic Violence Hotlines reached their highest monthly contact volume during the peak of the pandemic (Mineo, 2022).

These statistics indicate the trajectory of the consequences that public health measures have — despite being implemented to protect against the spread of the virus, they have had incidental effects on domestic violence rates. Lockdown measures heighten unemployment rates; these financial stressors are a significant risk factor for domestic abuse (Mineo, 2022). In addition, lockdown increases the amount of interaction time that occurs within the home. Normally, time outside — whether it be during employment hours or even time grocery shopping — gives those in risky relationships time to be apart from their partner. When lockdowns are enforced, this increases time together and exacerbates the potential for conflict. Furthermore, quarantine measures also reduce one's access to support systems. Isolation limits one's capacity to ask friends or family for help, or even make a phone call to a crisis helpline. This is evident as reports show that at the start of the pandemic, there was a decrease in the number of phone calls to crisis hotlines (Mineo, 2022). This decrease may be falsely attributed to rates of domestic violence decreasing. Rather, it is a result of decreased opportunities for victims of domestic violence to ask for help. Finally, the literature has shown that motions such as "Motions to Vacate the Marital Home" were considered to a lesser extent than in pre-pandemic times, as lockdown measures meant that there was decreased capacity to leave to the grocery store, much less temporarily vacate the home (Mineo, 2022). Within the justice system, the pandemic also made it more difficult to provide evidence due to the remote nature of courts, as documents are normally filed in person (Mineo, 2022). Overall, the COVID-19 pandemic has highlighted numerous gaps within our social systems that have exacerbated risk factors for victims of domestic violence during lockdown and quarantine measures.

Effect on Relationships and Divorce

The COVID-19 pandemic has also been seen to evoke a trend of increasing divorce rates. Despite divorce rates being on the rise since 2000, these numbers peaked in 2021 during the pandemic (Epstein & Associates, 2022). To support this, between July and October during the peak of the pandemic, a British law firm found a 122% increase in inquiries about divorce compared with the same period in the previous year (Savage, 2020). Charity Citizens Advice has also seen a huge spike in the number of searches for advice regarding ending a relationship (Savage, 2020).

Given these numbers, it seems to many that the pandemic has served as a perfect storm for relationships. Despite not being a direct causative factor for turmoil within relationships, it has served as a catalyst through a variety of factors. For one, a trend has been seen where there is an increase in how many females initiate divorce. Compared to 60% in the last year, 76% of divorce cases are initiated by female clients (Savage, 2020). This aligns with COVID-19 studies that have found that during the pandemic, despite both partners working from home in a heterosexual relationship, a disproportionate share of the housework and childcare is still done by women (Savage, 2020). Secondly, the COVID-19 pandemic has caused a massive rise in mental health issues that have served as a detriment to relationships (Savage, 2020). In addition, the pandemic and the associated public health measures such as lockdowns and quarantines have disrupted well-established routines for many. Not only did this result in partners spending increasing amounts of time together with little amounts of stimulation or support outside of their relationship, but it also resulted in a work-at-home transition

(Savage, 2020). This disruption in work-life balance increases the capacity for marital conflict that takes a heavy toll on a relationship and family. Beyond this, as children were also temporarily learning from home, this raised issues surrounding parenting. Parents that are usually at work and do not participate in some aspects of day-time parenting were suddenly thrust into these duties, and parents learned that there are many issues that they may not see eye-to-eye on (Epstein & Associates, 2022). These may include disagreements about meals, homework, and even COVID-19 vaccinations (Epstein & Associates, 2022). Finally, a major contributor to marital issues and consequently, divorce, has been money-related issues (Savage, 2020). The pandemic disproportionately hit those who were working in insecure employment such as within hospitality, leisure, retail, and tourism, leaving them without jobs. This subsequent decrease in household income can lead to conflict regarding different types of monetary consumption and psychological strain on couples that can greatly affect the relationship (Savage, 2020). Job loss has also been found to be especially difficult for men, who are more likely to base their self-esteem and worth on their ability to provide their families with financial stability (Savage, 2020).

Despite vaccine rollouts and lessening public health measures allowing life to start returning to how it was pre-pandemic, it is unclear as to whether this will halt the increase in divorce rates. The effect of the COVID-19 pandemic on the economy could result in a long-term recession, leading to longer-term money-related issues that strain marriages. In addition, psychotherapists have found that the pandemic has also sparked a re-evaluation within many people regarding their life decisions and emotional needs (Savage, 2020). After the pandemic, there has been an increase in the number of people that want to change their lifestyle, such as moving countries. It is likely that these re-evaluations and lifestyle changes will continue to affect marriages and relationships (Savage, 2020).

How the Pandemic Impacted Poverty

The COVID-19 pandemic has also had a significant impact on the burden of poverty worldwide. From 1990 to 2015, reports have shown that global poverty rates have been trending consistently downwards (World Relief, 2022). In fact, those at the extreme poverty level (living on approximately $1.90 every day) have gone from 36% to 10% (World Relief, 2022). Unfortunately, the recent pandemic has set the course of ending extreme poverty backward by approximately 3-4 years (World Relief, 2022). At the peak of the pandemic in 2020, an estimated 97 million more people were pushed over this poverty line (World Relief, 2022).

The public health measures and mass economic recession resulted in widespread unemployment rates. These unemployment rates were high throughout 2020 and slowly lowered while approaching the end of 2021 (Tracking the COVID-19 Economy's Effects on Food, Housing, and Employment Hardships, n.d.). However, at this time point, there were still 20 million households that reported food insecurity in the past 7 days and 10 million households that reported being behind on rent (Tracking the COVID-19 Economy's Effects on Food, Housing, and Employment Hardships, n.d.). During the earlier months of 2022, there were 3 million fewer people employed than prior to the pandemic in the United States alone (Tracking the COVID-19 Economy's Effects on Food, Housing, and Employment Hardships, n.d.).

These unemployment rates and the overall economic fallout have also disproportionately affected particular demographics during the pandemic. Specifically, Black people, Latino people, and other visible minorities have been on the brunt end of the pandemic's impacts. This provides deeper insight into the long-standing inequities rooted in structural racism, that the pandemic has magnified. Studies have found that Black and Latino adults were twice as likely as white adults to report food insecurity; in particular, the numbers are 17% for Black adults, 17% for Latino adults, and 6% for white adults (Tracking the COVID-19 Economy's Effects on Food, Housing, and Employment Hardships, n.d.). Additionally, people of color who rent also reported increased rates of renting insecurity and issues paying rent throughout the pandemic (Tracking the COVID-19 Economy's Effects on Food, Housing, and Employment

Hardships, n.d.). These same demographics have also been shown to recover far more slowly than white workers when it comes to job security and regaining employment opportunities (Tracking the COVID-19 Economy's Effects on Food, Housing, and Employment Hardships, n.d.).

These statistics are a testament to the fact that historical patterns of systemic racism continue to cycle back during periods of global turmoil, as the COVID-19 pandemic has shown. As a result, it is becoming increasingly important to protect these vulnerable populations that have been disproportionately affected by the pandemic. During the worst of the pandemic in 2020, some countries have implemented social protection programs that provide infrastructure to protect the very poor (Kharas & Dooley, 2021). Despite these only being temporary measures, it is hoped that they will provide the basic building blocks to permanently implement these protective programs to assist the poor and move them above the poverty line. Especially as technological developments have progressed significantly, these can assist governments in identifying and targeting groups that are in need (Kharas & Dooley, 2021).

The Impact of COVID-19 on Transnationalism

COVID-19 has also called attention to transnationalism and global solidarity throughout the global pandemic. The major disruption of various transnational infrastructures provides insight into the consequences on transnationally mobile groups and how fragile the global network truly is. There are a variety of factors that interplay to threaten the well-being and security of the transnationally mobile throughout the pandemic. Firstly, travel channels have been vastly impacted by border closures and surveillance software. At the start of the pandemic, there were a total of 111,000 travel restrictions and border closures reported globally (Benton et al., 2021). Some countries such as those of European Union member states maintained travel channels to allow selective migration across borders (Benton et al., 2021). However, other countries such as Australia and China have closed their borders almost entirely (Benton et al., 2021). Borders have gained additional fortification infrastructure, including quarantine measures for travelers, mobility surveillance and location tracking, and more. These interruptions in routine border control policies have interrupted various mobility infrastructures; this includes but is not limited to transport, communication, and brokerage. In fact, almost 200 European airports are facing potential closures now (United Nations News, 2021). Beyond infrastructure alone, those employed within the travel space such as airlines and travel agents have experienced obsolescence during the pandemic. These disruptions have not only resulted in mass job insecurity but also affected the exchange of necessary medical equipment abroad (i.e., COVID-19 vaccines, and personal protective equipment) (Felter, 2021). Finally, resource competition has proven to be a major issue for low- and middle-income countries that face extreme inequities in obtaining medical resources (Nehring & Hu, 2022). Given the shortage of resources worldwide, poorer nations experience exacerbated global inequalities as richer nations secure significantly greater quantities of lifesaving medical resources.

During the pandemic, transnationally mobile groups have been disproportionately affected by closures and disruptions in transnational infrastructures. This has greatly affected their well-being and survival. Firstly, transnational immobility due to border closures and public health measures have resulted in these groups being forced to stay where they are. For some, this meant long periods of separation between family members; for others, this jeopardized monetary sustenance for those who relied on crossing borders (Nehring & Hu, 2022). In addition, almost 80 million refugees are stranded in various disasters during this time, exposing these groups to not only physical violence but also potentially racial abuse (WHO, 2020). Beyond this, many individuals rely on travel to practice self-development and progression. For example, massive numbers of international students were unable to begin their studies abroad due to travel restrictions (Nehring & Hu, 2022). Finally, transnational groups also experienced heightened COVID-19 infection and mortality levels (Nehring & Hu, 2022). As national protective responses are normally citizen-centered, economic and structural support for non-citizen groups was largely neglected.

The pandemic has highlighted the importance of transnational solidarity throughout catastrophic global events, as a means of protecting those caught between nations. The consequences inflicted on vulnerable populations during this time serve as an urgent reminder to protect these groups through transnational social protection infrastructure.

Conclusion

The COVID-19 pandemic has magnified downstream socio cultural consequences that have been a result of economic, political, and social fallout. It is integral to examine these issues that may otherwise be brushed under the rug, as not only have particular nations and minorities been disproportionately affected by the pandemic, but there have also been long-lasting impacts on social issues such as poverty and domestic violence. This highlights the importance of preventative planning and developing protective programs for the most vulnerable.

References

Baloch, S., Baloch, M. A., Zheng, T., & Pei, X. (2020). The Coronavirus Disease 2019 (COVID-19) Pandemic. The Tohoku Journal of Experimental Medicine, 250(4), 271–278. https://doi.org/10.1620/tjem.250.271

Banerjee, D., & Meena, K. S. (2021). COVID-19 as an "Infodemic" in Public Health: Critical Role of the Social Media. Frontiers in Public Health, 9. https://www.frontiersin.org/articles/10.3389/fpubh.2021.610623

Benton M, Batalova J, Davidoff-Gore S, et al. (2021) COVID-19 and the State of Global Mobility in 2020. Geneva: International Organization for Migration and Migration Policy Institute. Available at: https://www.iom.int/news/first-comprehensive-global-analysis-covid-19-travel-restrictions-border-closures-weighs-future

Epstein & Associates. Why the Pandemic Caused a Spike in Divorces. (2022, May 18). Epstein & Associates. https://www.epsteinlawyers.com/why-the-pandemic-caused-a-spike-in-divorces/

Felter C (2021) A Guide to Global COVID-19 Vaccine Efforts. Available at: https://www.cfr.org/backgrounder/guide-global-covid-19-vaccine-efforts

Hu Z, Yang Z, Li Q, Zhang A. The COVID-19 infodemic: infodemiology study analyzing stigmatizing search terms. J Med Internet Res. (2020) 22:e22639. doi: 10.2196/22639

Kharas, H., & Dooley, M. (2021, June 2). Long-run impacts of COVID-19 on extreme poverty. Brookings. https://www.brookings.edu/blog/future-development/2021/06/02/long-run-impacts-of-covid-19-on-extreme-poverty/

Mansouri, F. (2020, May 29). The socio-cultural implications of COVID-19 | UNESCO. UNESCO. https://www.unesco.org/en/articles/socio-cultural-implications-covid-19

Mineo, L. (2022, June 29). 'Shadow pandemic' of domestic violence. Harvard Gazette. https://news.harvard.edu/gazette/story/2022/06/shadow-pandemic-of-domestic-violence/

Muralidar, S., Ambi, S. V., Sekaran, S., & Krishnan, U. M. (2020). The emergence of COVID-19 as a global pandemic: Understanding the epidemiology, immune response and potential therapeutic targets of SARS-CoV-2. Biochimie, 179, 85–100. https://doi.org/10.1016/j.biochi.2020.09.018

Nehring, D., & Hu, Y. (2022). COVID-19, Nation-States and Fragile Transnationalism. Sociology, 56(1), 183–190. https://doi.org/10.1177/00380385211033729

Savage, M. (2020, December 6). Why the pandemic is causing spikes in break-ups and divorces. https://www.bbc.com/worklife/article/20201203-why-the-pandemic-is-causing-spikes-in-break-ups-and-divorces

Tracking the COVID-19 Economy's Effects on Food, Housing, and Employment Hardships. (n.d.). Center on Budget and Policy Priorities. Retrieved from https://www.cbpp.org/research/poverty-and-inequality/tracking-the-covid-19-economys-effects-on-food-housing-and

United Nations News (2021) Air Travel Down 60 Per Cent, As Airline Industry Losses Top $370 Billion: ICAO. Available at: https://news.un.org/en/story/2021/01/1082302

Wassler, P., & Talarico, C. (2021). Sociocultural impacts of COVID-19: A social representations perspective. Tourism Management Perspectives, 38, 100813. https://doi.org/10.1016/j.tmp.2021.100813

World Health Organization (2020) Migrants and Refugees Say COVID-19 has Dramatically Worsened Their Lives. Available at: https://www.who.int/news-room/feature-stories/detail/migrants-and-refugees-say-covid-19-has-dramatically-worsened-their-lives

World Relief. COVID-19 Impact on the World's Poor. (2022, March 15). World Relief. https://worldrelief.org/covid-report/

Chapter 3
Education: The nature of teaching and learning post pandemic

By Ryan Baxter

Introduction

The transition to distance and online learning models at the onset of the Covid-19 pandemic came with many challenges, including those of access to connection, ill-equipped administrators and educators, social isolation, lack of confidence in building meaningful relationships in the online environment, increased screen time, and questions of authenticity and assessment of learning. Conversely, many opportunities and affordances of online education became apparent, including the building of community among disparate and separated learners and groups, the possibility of immediate formative assessment and frequent feedback, and greater student motivation resulting from self-regulated learning, individual choice, and learner agency. There is consensus in both academic and non-academic literature that education has changed permanently because of the pandemic experience.

In the early days of the pandemic, conversations in education focused mainly on high-level questions about how the pandemic would disrupt education (Weishaar, n.d.). These concerns generally concentrated on practical elements rather than the learning and student experience (Weishaar, n.d.), but have now evolved into more distinct, interconnected thematic categories of education-related problems that have been highlighted by the pandemic, and what opportunities must be acted upon post pandemic. This chapter offers an introduction to the themes of instructional design, shifting educational and institutional priorities, mental health and reflective practices, social inequality, and faculty development. None of these ideas are new in education; all were in motion pre-pandemic, but have been accelerated, changed, or highlighted through the pandemic experience. They have become central in conversations and research about the post-pandemic educational landscape. This chapter focuses on the impact of the pandemic and the future of higher education, but most themes and ideas are also highly applicable to public education. Some ideas that are specific or relevant to K-12 education are detailed.

Instructional Design

The first major theme is the importance and nature of instructional design. Instructional design refers to the analysis of learning problems, and the design, development, implementation, and evaluation of processes and resources that improve learning and learning environments (Reiser & Dempsey, 2018). Instructional designers use processes, models, and design techniques to employ instructional media, with appropriate and considerate use of technology and digital tools (Reiser & Dempsey, 2018). The pandemic has highlighted the importance of this field and its contributions to our understanding and experience of the differences between in-person and online/digital learning environments. Further, Universal Design for Learning (UDL), which is a key design principle in education, has experienced greater engagement because of the pandemic experience and will be focused on more strongly post pandemic. UDL in many ways encourages constructivist, even connectivist, learning environments through its principles of multiple means of representation, engagement, and action and expression (CAST, 2020).

While constructivism as a learning theory and set of practices continues to evolve, the pandemic experience of distance teaching and learning has demonstrated its value and increased the momentum of its effect on education (Ilardo & Cuconato, 2022). Higher education as a whole and its instructional environments can be open spaces where knowledge and expertise are exchanged and combined from several different sources and resources by students, cooperating with academic and non-academic professionals as they construct knowledge, experiences, skills, and attitudes that are meaningful to them (Ilardo & Cuconato, 2022). Accompanying this more developed understanding of constructivism is increased intentional thinking about the use of technology in teaching higher order thinking skills (Ilardo & Cuconato, 2022). This was not without error though, as significant decisions about technology practices are still frequently made on the basis that they are technical rather than pedagogical, cultural, or ethical in nature (Carozza & Gennaro, 2021).

Returning to UDL, accessibility is a key component of this approach to design. Some adaptations to teaching and learning during the pandemic helped students with disabilities, but other adaptations only created more barriers (Lash, 2021). While there is still a serious lack of faculty training and awareness of disability and accessibility in higher education, the pandemic experience has highlighted accessibility as a matter of both instructional design and social equity, and the reality that proactive models are superior to the reactive ones which are most common today. Solutions for the future include increased faculty training and development on disability, accessibility, and technology use in teaching and learning, as well as clearer institutional policies about how to support students with disabilities when major disruptions to usual teaching and learning occur (Lash, 2021). The pandemic highlighted that advances towards equity are often lost during crises, and students with disabilities were one student population that was caught off guard, with no clear plan to support them in their unique challenges (Lash, 2021). Proactive and accessible instructional design are key elements in addressing accessibility in education post-pandemic.

In conclusion, despite the rigidity of most higher education systems, the pandemic has shown that academia can be quite flexible when required, even using trial and error to quickly devise new teaching and learning approaches. The pandemic forced many educators for the first time to ask themselves two of the most important instructional design questions: "what is it I really want to teach, and what is the best way to teach it based on the learning environment and learner population?"

Shifting Educational Priorities

Pre-pandemic, higher education had begun to focus more on the challenges of promoting employability post-graduation and social cohesion within and beyond the campus environments, and the pandemic has accelerated this trend (Ilardo & Cuconato, 2022). Today's learners require lifelong learning skills for both work and leisure areas of life, and this is driving new instructional priorities and techniques in higher education, including the constructivist principles and techniques mentioned above (Ilardo & Cuconato, 2022). Universities and colleges have long known that knowledge-based syllabi and curriculum are no longer entirely adequate, but the pandemic experience is accelerating the move away from these models to those that better value and incorporate higher-order learning and employable skills for students. Students also require stronger skills with information and communication technologies to interact with and understand the impact of digitization on their work and contemporary society, culture, and politics (Ilardo & Cuconato, 2022). This digital aspect has been highlighted by the collective pandemic experience, including educational, cultural, and political elements. Additionally, the pandemic has highlighted the importance of models that can support and value on-demand or in-the-moment learning opportunities both in the classroom and online (Carozza & Gennaro, 2021).

Coupled to this is a reality that more people than ever have access to higher education, further diversifying both the student populations in higher education and the necessary instructional formats. In the fastest-growing institutions, the only way to accommodate such large numbers of learners is to embrace hybrid and distance education. A greater variety of programs is needed, with instructional approaches, learning experiences, and supports that can address the distinct needs (personal, academic, and economic), interests, goals, and cultural backgrounds of individual students and the groups they form (Ilardo & Cuconato, 2022). Post-pandemic, the strategic and long-term priorities of higher education institutions will shift faster than they did pre-pandemic, particularly in the proportions of in-person, hybrid, and online learning being offered, as well as the focus on addressing student needs outside of the classroom.

Mental Health and Reflective Practice

The pandemic made student mental health visible in new ways and revealed implications for both teaching and learning post-pandemic and teacher-student relationships (Blewett & Ebben, 2021). It has accelerated movements that encourage teachers and faculty to pay greater attention to student mental health and their understanding of it (Blewett & Ebben, 2021). Post-pandemic, student mental health will be understood as a matter of equity in higher education, further driving the move towards universal design for learning in courses and learning environments (Blewett & Ebben, 2021). This can go beyond universal design to trauma-informed teaching and critical grief pedagogy, which are both mindsets and tools that can bring greater humanity to higher education in the context of the collective trauma and grief experienced during and after the pandemic (Blewett & Ebben, 2021). Students have experienced loneliness, isolation, and social anxiety, and readjustment to more usual learning models and social interactions will take time (Weishaar, n.d.).

Post-pandemic, most higher education systems and institutions will be making hybrid and online learning environments a greater part of their strategy and experience. Building a humane and ethical digital environment that employs an ethics of care in course design and delivery is essential to creating transformative learning experiences in digital spaces (Carozza & Gennaro, 2021) (similar to the educational priorities described above, instructional design is central in this process). The surveillance of students' online activities during the pandemic highlighted the very explicit nature of higher education's academic honesty and integrity concerns, and the socio-economic divides that occur during invigilated and statutory assessments (Carozza & Gennaro, 2021). A community of trust, rather than mistrust, should be fostered, and the necessity of examination-style assessments questioned. Teaching and designing with compassion post-pandemic will require a more universal and accessible instructional design, radical dialogue in the online environment, and a willingness to extend deadlines and/or use deadline windows (Carozza & Gennaro, 2021). This pedagogy of compassion revolves around inclusion, equity, and social justice, where students have greater autonomy, better understand their learning as a process of personal growth, and can more effectively develop their relationships with the learning content and each other (Carozza & Gennaro, 2021).

Higher education is also moving towards more reflective and reflexive curricula for programs, enabling students to develop deeper and more effective learning skills, to devise new methods of reasoning, and to improve their creativity in problem solving (Ilardo & Cuconato, 2022). Part of this reflexivity is an increased critical consciousness of social injustices (Carozza & Gennaro, 2021). Students become constructors of their learning as they engage in answering the very questions they ask in the classroom, especially those related to justice. There is now greater movement towards humanity and care in education, and the prioritization of student identity, which aids in the calling out and naming of injustices, and in creating space for previously marginalized or silenced voices (Lewis, Maas, & Allsup, 2022). Teachers and faculty are now also encouraged to adopt reflexive approaches to teaching and to be more aware of the implicit attitudes, beliefs, and knowledge systems that guide their daily and institutional activities (Ilardo & Cuconato, 2022).

There is some cultural resistance to these ideas of critical pedagogy, humane teaching, reflective practices, and prioritization of student mental health. In reality, a truly inclusive and equitable higher education system that has justice, reflection, and mental health at its center will take years to root (Blewett & Ebben, 2021). While many faculty may still be anxious about maintaining professional boundaries around student mental health, there is greater recognition now that students are people first, and learners second. The pandemic spurred pedagogical innovations and flexibility by systems, educators, and learners, generating skills and attitudes that will aid in this profound shift in perspective and action around student mental health (Blewett & Ebben, 2021). Despite the challenges, a critical mass has been moved and a pedagogy of compassion will destabilize the traditional teacher-knows-best methodology and create a more equal power dynamic both in the classroom and online (Carozza & Gennaro, 2021).

Social Inequality

As alluded to in the previous section, one of the long-term impacts of the pandemic is the revealing of educational inequalities (Bradbury, 2021). The nature of at-home learning highlighted the social inequalities among different student groups and the extent to which public school systems serve as a branch of social services in the community (Bradbury, 2021). Additionally, the pandemic experience is being used by some as justification for the over-datafication of public education, including the quantification of student experiences and interactions (Bradbury, 2021). One danger in this overdatafication is that 'unquantifiable' teaching approaches and methods, such as in-classroom constructivist learning, start to look inefficient or wasteful. Underlying these complex issues of educational inequality and datafication is the unfortunate elision of two ideas: that poverty and lack of merit are synonymous (Bradbury, 2021). Too often, socio-economically disadvantaged students are assumed to be of lesser potential than their advantaged peers, and this discourse remains seriously hard to challenge despite the pandemic experience, in part because disadvantaged students have suffered the greatest educational losses. Without their physical schools being able to offer targeted social support, these student groups fall further behind, and there is risk that attempting to quantify every element of their learning will only further reinforce outdated ideas that they are destined to be disadvantaged indefinitely (Bradbury, 2021).

Post-pandemic, a focus on children's emotional strength and resilience, the use of trauma-informed practice, and environments that value student collaboration instead of competition can all advance social wellbeing in schools, and are necessary to recovery for schools and students (Bradbury, 2021). While these ideas are targeted towards public education, similar challenges do occur in higher education as well, where many disadvantaged students had difficulty accessing the support systems that higher education institutions provide on campus.

Faculty Development

Faculty development has been a common thread through many of the themes identified in this chapter, including instructional design, accessibility, and reflective practice. The pandemic forced faculty to interrogate philosophies and practices that had gone unchallenged in their practice for decades, and this trend must continue. Many educators responded with innovative teaching approaches that humanized their pedagogy and made experiences more relevant and meaningful for their students (i.e., they improved their instructional designs based on the learning context and mode) (Lewis, Maas, & Allsup, 2022). Further, many students became the instructors, demonstrating their knowledge of specific tools and ways of learning with technology (Lewis, Maas, & Allsup, 2022). Post-pandemic, educators, administration, and faculty who train future educators have opportunities to be positive forces of disruption, always nudging themselves and students into discomfort, challenging their thinking, imagining new possibilities, and avoiding complacency (Lewis, Maas, & Allsup, 2022).

These opportunities for faculty development come with both practical and social challenges. Teachers often felt ignored when decisions were made during the pandemic, which has caused exhaustion and demoralization that continues into the post-pandemic era (Weishaar, n.d.). While the experience has demonstrated that teachers are capable of innovation, the pandemic has left many too tired to take on new initiatives and continue experimenting upon the return to classroom learning (Weishaar, n.d.). In higher education, exceptional workloads are a barrier to development. One potential solution is a rethinking of how educator time and talents are distributed in education systems. The introduction to new ways of teaching and learning has broadened the perspective on how teachers can better apply their strengths in their positions;

there is potential for educators to be matched to the environments which best match their strengths (Hess, 2022), potentially combating burnout from the pandemic. Some imagine a school system where education is more hybridized, and educators teach what and where they are most effective, rather than being forced into the typical roles which require them to spend significant time attending to other, non-teaching tasks.

Other Themes

Two other sub-themes have emerged in the discussion of post-pandemic education. Firstly, there is research suggesting that the pandemic experience has increased public awareness and consciousness of climate change (Brown & Luzmore, 2021). Many families have chosen to move away from urban centers to areas with more green space and natural environment because of their lockdown experiences, and these transitions show some evidence of replication in school environments. Outdoor learning, forest schools, and environment-based education are not only now seen as more desirable, but necessary in society's struggle against climate change.

Secondly, the pandemic saw an unprecedented rise in fake news, misinformation, and political polarization around public health issues and the news media (Brown & Luzmore, 2021). There are numerous approaches that can be adopted in school systems post-pandemic to counter the 'post-truth' movement, where emotional appeal and belief have greater influence than fact in shaping public opinion and policy (Brown & Luzmore, 2021). Firstly, a focus on the teaching of values and skills in schools, including honesty, accountability, and research skills that assess the reliability of information is needed. Secondly, students should be introduced to methods and resources that debunk fake news, helping them separate what is true from what is not. Thirdly, teaching the art of rhetoric can help students state their ideas and facts in ways that attend appropriately to rational and emotional imperatives. These sub-themes of environment and truth demonstrate that post-pandemic educational priorities are equally valid for adult life and workplace contexts as they are for public education.

Conclusion

The major themes presented in this chapter on the future of education post pandemic included the importance of instructional design (including constructivist learning, accessibility, and universal design for learning), shifting education priorities (including new direction for curriculum, use of technology in teaching, and student needs outside the classroom), mental health and reflective practice (including issues of equity, humane teaching and learning, and reflexive practices). Additionally, there are unique challenges and opportunities that underlie these thematic categories, including social inequalities, faculty and educator development, and societal trends around climate change and the nature of truth. Most importantly, these thematic areas are deeply interconnected.

There are three potential trajectories for post-pandemic education, both in public and higher education: a return to the pre-pandemic status quo, a focus on remediating the learning losses occurred during the pandemic, or an effort to reinvent education in a humane way that focuses on building the self-regulatory skills students gained through the pandemic experience (Weishaar, n.d.). Ideally, the latter of these three will prevail, resulting in a public and higher education systems that are improved over pre-pandemic models for teaching, learning, and the wellbeing of students and educators.

This chapter has focused mainly on themes which are applicable to higher education contexts in the Western context. It is important to recognize that public and higher education worldwide has been affected by the nature of teaching and learning during the pandemic, and is therefore experiencing similar post-pandemic challenges, opportunities, and changes. It seems appropriate to close this chapter with a brief summary of UNESCO's (United Nations Educational, Scientific, and Cultural Organization) nine ideas for public action for education in a post-covid world (International Commission, 2020). The document emphasizes that experiences of hybrid learning across the world are not equal and that school systems provide social services for millions of children around the world. These nine ideas for public action invite debate, engagement, and action by governments, education professionals, researchers, and learners (International Commission, 2020):

1. Commit to strengthening education as a common good, seeing education as a defense against inequality.
2. Expand the definition of the right to education to address the importance of connectivity and access to information.
3. Value the teaching profession and teacher collaboration.
4. Promote student, youth, and children's participation and rights in their education.
5. Protect and value the social spaces that physical schools provide.
6. Make free and open-source technologies available to teachers and students, including open educational resources and open access digital tools.
7. Ensure scientific literacy within curricula, particularly as we struggle against misinformation and the denial of scientific knowledge.
8. Protect domestic and international financing of public education.
9. Advance global solidarity to end current levels of inequality.

References

Blewett, L. & Ebben, M. (2021). Post-pandemic anxiety: Teaching and learning for student mental wellness in communication. In J. M. Valenzano (Ed.) Post-pandemic pedagogy: A paradigm shift (chapter 7). Lexington Books.

Bradbury, A. (2021). Ability, inequality and post-pandemic schools: rethinking contemporary myths of meritocracy. Policy Press.

Brown, C. & Luzmore, R. (2021) Educating tomorrow: Learning for the post-pandemic world (1st edition). Emerald Publishing Limited.

Carozza, L. & Gennaro, S. (2021). Post-pandemic pedagogy: Compassionate and caring course curriculum in the digital university. In J. M. Valenzano (Ed.) Post-pandemic pedagogy: A paradigm shift (chapter 3). Lexington Books.

Center for Applied Special Technology (CAST). (2020). The UDL Guidelines. https://udlguidelines.cast.org/?utm_source=castsite&lutm_medium=web&utm_campaign=none&utm_content=aboutudl.

Hess, F. M (2022). Education after the pandemic. National Affairs. https://nationalaffairs.com/publications/detail/education-after-the-pandemic.

Ilardo, M. & Cuconato, M. (2022). Rethinking academic teaching at and beyond the pandemic. In S.

Gonçalves & S. Majhanovich (Eds.), Pandemic, disruption and adjustment in higher education (chapter 10). Brill.

International Commission on the Futures of Education (2020). Education in a post-COVID world: Nine ideas for public action. Paris, UNESCO.

Lash, B. N. (2021). The pandemic and disability inclusive pedagogy: Examining the response to covid-19 in higher education. In J. M. Valenzano (Ed.) Post-pandemic pedagogy: A paradigm shift (chapter 8). Lexington Books.

Lewis, J., Maas, A., & Allsup, R. E. (2022). Music education on the verge: stories of pandemic teaching and transformative change (J. Lewis & A. Maas, Eds.). Lexington Books.

Reiser, R. A. & Dempsey, J. V., (Eds.) (2018). Trends and issues in instructional design and technology (4th edition). Pearson.

Weishaar, K. (n.d.). Reinventing education post-pandemic. MIT Teaching + Learning Lab. https://tll.mit.edu/reinventing-education-post-pandemic/.

Chapter 4
Post-pandemic lessons on inclusivity: Aftermath of vulnerable populations and how to move forward

By Amal Rizvi

As of November 2022, it has been over 2 years since the World Health Organization declared the COVID-19 pandemic. Since then, it has been a tumultuous ride as people learned to navigate society once again - this time, with new regulations set in place. In many ways, the pandemic united societies. For instance, measures like masking and getting vaccinated are most effective if people participate collectively. This collective agreement to protect each other's health by exhibiting compliance with rules set by governments represents a basal level of empathy people have for one another, and that empathy is a beautiful thing. However, it is important to remember that not everyone had governments, institutions, and communities standing by their side during the COVID-19 pandemic.

In Canada, approximately 22% of the population who are aged 15 or higher have one or more disabilities (Morris et al., 2018). Similarly, the Centers for Disease Control and Prevention (CDC) states that 26% of adults in the United States are living with a disability (2022). Disability is loosely thought of as being restricted or unable to complete tasks or activities at the level considered normal for the general population (Mewes et al., 2009). While this definition provides a good basis, one must remember that disability does not exist in a vacuum. Rather, disability comes to light when one's apparent inability to perform in a certain way is unsupported by the environment they are in (Institute of Medicine, 1997). In North America, there is an evident dominant culture in terms of how societies operate. It is elements of this culture that directly shape the environment people live in.

While countless hours have been spent developing policies and procedures for North Americans adapting to COVID-19, much of these developments were only made with the dominant culture in mind, and thus, they were inherently discriminatory against people living with disabilities (Lund & Ayers, 2022). Two years since the declaration of the COVID-19 pandemic, one may ask, "Why does any of this matter now?". While it seems true that the commotion surrounding the COVID-19 pandemic seems to be waning with time, the issues faced by people living with disabilities during the pandemic continue to be relevant today. Much of the discrimination imposed on this population during the pandemic will continue if policymakers do not reflect on their own incorrect perceptions of people living with disabilities, and aim to abolish these perceptions in light of growth. This growth may consequently lead to improvements in attitudes and policies made by lawmakers that can make navigating the healthcare system easier for vulnerable populations.

The aim of this chapter is to highlight the lessons on inclusivity learned during the COVID-19 pandemic, with respect to the two categories aforementioned: i) attitudes towards people living with disabilities, and ii) regulations that excluded them. Incorrect and discriminatory attitudes coupled with unjust policies facilitate the intentional segregation of disabled people from society. This segregation is what prevents people living with disabilities from accessing the infrastructure, resources, and support they need to thrive in a world that was not built with them in mind. While these two categories are nowhere near enough to cover all of the lessons on inclusivity that the pandemic has brought to light, this section is meant to serve as an introduction to raise awareness and spark meaningful discussion that can, hopefully, incite positive changes in communities.

Negative attitudes regarding people living with disabilities that shaped the COVID-19 healthcare response

It is no secret that, unfortunately, prejudice towards people living with disabilities exists today. Perhaps more important to realize is that this prejudice is nowhere near a new development; rather, it has been a consistent observation throughout history. In Ancient Greece, Spartans, who were known to normalize characteristics such as strength and masculinity, people who were physically incapable of demonstrating these characteristics were scrutinized (Penrose, 2015). In fact, Spartans mandated infanticide - the killing of infants - for children who were deemed too weak or deformed, as per their standards (Tooley, 1972). What was the basis of this negative attitude towards children with disabilities? The answer is somewhat unclear, but it likely stemmed from the idea that children born physically abnormal would not be able to contribute to the Spartan community. With Sparta being a society of warriors and placing great importance on their army, it may have been assumed that people living with disabilities simply did not "fit in", for lack of better words.

Despite the fact that the ancient Greeks lived and died many years ago, this idea of being unable to contribute to society, and thus being dismissed in lieu of matters that seem more important, is something that exists in society today. Just recently in Toronto, Ontario, a news report outlining the medically assisted death of Michael Fraser circulated through the media outlets. Fraser was disabled, unable to work, and was only receiving $1,100 per month in Canadian dollars to survive (Phillips, 2022). With the lack of support forcing him into poverty, Fraser saw little reason to continue living and was approved for MAiD - medical assistance in dying. One may ask, "How does this situation parallel the ancient Greeks' infanticide of disabled children?". Well, similar to the ancient Greeks, Fraser was never provided enough government support to manage his disabilities and live a fruitful life. Instead, he was cast aside by government and local agencies. While there are multiple factors that contributed to the situation, one thing is clear: nobody prioritized Fraser's wellbeing until it was too late. One thousand dollars per month in this economy is chump change for a Torontonian, and organizations must know this. So why would they provide this to a man living with severe disabilities, and think it was enough to help him? Did they even want to help him? Did they see value in helping him? These are all questions that come to mind, and highlight the ridiculous level of discrimination and ignorance regarding the matters of some of the city's most vulnerable people.

This now begs the question: were these same negative attitudes and prejudices present in the COVID-19 healthcare response? The answer is, unfortunately, yes. During the pandemic, much of the legislation made by governments to protect citizens was made without people living with disabilities in mind. Mandatory orders, such as masking, did not account for the fact that some people may need to read lips, for instance? Where were the mandates for masks with clear panels to facilitate this? Where was the consideration for physically disabled people when stay at home orders and mandatory curfews prevented them from accessing the personnel and supplies they needed?

Statistically, it was obvious that people living with disabilities needed support. Given this, ignorance does not seem like a valid argument anymore. Rather, the more blatant answer, the one that is most undesirable for people to face because it highlights their ugly nature, is prejudice.

Why do policy makers create health regulations that seem to deliberately exclude people living with disabilities? The likely answer is that they do not view their lives as equivalent to those of people they deem normal. Many people have the misconception that people with disabilities can not live a full, long life; they assume that disability means being subjected to bedrest until one rots away. For this reason, it is likely that people who make these policies are assuming that people with significant disabilities will not survive COVID-19 to begin with, so there is no point in supporting them through it. It is a gruesome, disgusting thought, to assume someone's life is not worth enough to protect. However, it reflects the treatment that people with disabilities have been dealt with throughout history, so perhaps it is not that surprising after all.

While past actions of people who made policies that excluded people living with disabilities cannot be forgotten, one of the best things that can be done at this point is to highlight some of the crucial lessons learned during the pandemic, as a result of policy makers shortcomings.

The first major lesson policy makers must learn and implement into their future work is the concepts of equality versus equity. Policies that are rooted in equality involve the equal treatment of all people, with no regard for their unique needs or circumstances (Nedha, 2011). While on the surface, there may not seem to be anything wrong with equality, aiming for equality rather than equity can facilitate the erasure of people's needs on the individual level. It is equal policies that have facilitated much of the isolation people living with disabilities experienced during the pandemic. On the other hand, equity is aiming for an equal level of success for all people while treating people differently based on their unique needs (Nedha, 2011). It is recommended that policies are revised to ensure that people living with disabilities have equitable opportunity to access the resources they need.

A second lesson stems from the fact that much of the language used during the COVID-19 pandemic to describe the state of the world was inherently discriminatory. Phrases like "We will all get through this together!" might seem like motivational words of encouragement when said by our country's leaders. However, it is necessary to realize that these words can seem tone-deaf and dismissive to individuals who live with disabilities, as they may be more negatively impacted by the reeling effects of the pandemic. By glossing over their situation and, again, equating their experience to that of everyone else, the unique circumstances they face are ignored. A simple change in language shifts the entire attitude, and thus, opens up a huge realm of possible solutions for the issues that people with disabilities face.

A third major lesson that can be learned from the pandemic is checking one's own privilege. Throughout the pandemic, many people suffered immensely. Jobs were lost, schools were canceled, money was tight, and social interactions were far and few in between. However, undoubtedly, some people suffered worse than others. Moving forward, it is crucial that abled individuals keep people with disabilities in mind during large scale issues, check in with them, and attempt to use their privilege to assist them. For example, if an able-bodied individual is able to leave the house with a mask on to purchase groceries, there is no harm in asking their neighbor with a disability if they need anything. Why? Because the able-bodied individual has the privilege of safely going out, while following health guidelines, without as large of a risk. If more people recognize their privilege in society and use it to help those who do not have it, more people living with disabilities may have the opportunity to access resources that abled individuals take for granted every day.

Negative attitudes directed towards people living with disabilities are not uncommon, and not a new occurrence. The COVID-19 pandemic served as a much overdue learning opportunity for policy makers and everyday citizens alike to check own privilege, become more cognizant of their language, and strive for a more equitable approach to policies and regulations, society could begin to show the seeds of a more just world for people living with disabilities.

Regulations made during the COVID-19 pandemic that exclude people living with disabilities

The COVID-19 pandemic brought forth new regulations, policies, and emergency planning that were not in place prior to the situation. However, as with other international emergencies, people living with disabilities were - rather transparently - excluded (White, 2022). As with other matters pertaining to people with disabilities, this is not an isolated issue. In fact, people with disabilities have been historically left behind in other emergencies worldwide; they are more likely than able-bodied people to be abandoned during floods, earthquakes, and wars (Battle, 2014). Some of the ways in which this occurred, both literally and metaphorically, throughout the pandemic are outlined below.

First, masks were rather symbolic of the COVID-19 pandemic (White, 2022). With mask mandates enforced throughout the entire world in nearly every public setting, the spread of COVID was significantly reduced; masks were a protective measure that minimized COVID risk to people at large, but especially people living with disabilities, who were at a much higher risk to begin with. However, as the world gets back on track and society starts to "go back to normal" (in reality, society is not normal at all; COVID risk is still high and vulnerable people are equally as vulnerable), the same mandates that were put in place to protect some of the country's most vulnerable populations have been abolished. Some may argue that it is people with disabilities' responsibility to take ownership of their own health; however, this argument reinforces the marginalization that the disabled community faces. Why should one community of people be forced to handle a difficult situation on their own, while everyone else goes about their lives in a way that is harmful? Why must people living with disability navigate this unprecedented situation alone, without anyone else on their team?

Similarly, forcing people to come into work when they have tested positive for COVID-19 is another move that directly harms people living with disability (White, 2022). Policies enforced in workplaces make it so employees who are ill may not get the same paid time off that they once did during the peak of the pandemic. In a world where money is tight and the risk of unemployment is a real possibility rather than a distant thought, employees feel like they need to choose between their health and their job. This harms people with disabilities in two ways: i) if they themselves are ill, they must come into work and not allow their bodies to recover, and ii) other people who come in to work with COVID can easily transmit the virus to them. The solution to this very simple problem would be to re-evaluate the pay system and ensure that people who are ill have the opportunity to prioritize their own and other's health without an underlying fear of losing money. Paying employees fair wages, providing paid sick days, and being more empathetic towards people when they are ill - not only with COVID, but with other conditions as well - is a step in the right direction.

Mental health disability is a third major issue that COVID-19 policies simply did not address during the pandemic (Public Service Alliance of Canada [PSAC], 2020). Mental health disabilities are common among the disabled population, and can be exacerbated from the stress of the global pandemic. With stay at home orders keeping people indoors, confusing messaging in the media that may not be accessible to people living with disabilities in the first place, financial stressors and lack of uncertainty, many members of the disabled community have reported that their mental health has declined during the pandemic. Within the disabled community, substance abuse has increased during the pandemic, as have suicide rates. Here, it is crucial to reinforce that mental health disabilities intersect with other social determinants of health, such as gender, race, social status, and educational background. While mental health in general has been increasing within the disabled community, members of this community who, for instance, identify as female or are racialized have been more greatly affected.

What have governments done to address this situation? The short answer is, "Not enough". It seems that the Canadian government has not directly addressed any of the disparities that people with mental health disabilities have faced during the pandemic. Again, many policy makers have taken the "We are all in this together" approach to the situation, and blatantly ignore the unique circumstances that make disabled persons' experience with mental health completely different and multifaceted. People living with disabilities still have limited access to mental health support. It is on governments and policy makers to address this and provide support as needed. Whether this is in the form of cash transfers so people can afford services, or simply making services more accessible, unfair policies that gatekeep these services must be re-examined.

What lesson has been learned from all of this, one might ask? Governments, policy makers, and people in power have been either endorsing discriminatory policies that put people with disabilities at risk, or have not been doing enough to create equitable opportunity for them to drive. Moving forward, emergency planning needs to be done with people with disabilities in mind. It is not enough to create general policies and expect every single group to follow with ease. Rather, policies need to be discussed in depth with a round table of people from multiple populations and backgrounds before they are set in stone and made public. People living with disabilities need a seat at the table in order to be heard and facilitate the implementation of policies that benefit them.

Conclusion: Many lessons have been learned, but there is still more work to do

While this chapter has discussed two angles from which lessons regarding disability inclusiveness have been brought to light, the battle does not end here. For the world to become more inclusive to people living with disabilities, entire systems need to be overhauled and reconstructed. Society was founded upon the exclusion of groups deemed less important to the majority culture, and thus, disablism pollutes every facet of society today; whether it is institutions, social circles, or policies. Vulnerable populations need to be brought into the conversation, not as vague, impersonal objects, but as contributors who can voice their point of view and shed light on issues they face.

If there is one lesson that the pandemic has taught society, it is that unexpected global emergencies are indeed a possibility. While it may not be possible to predict every single natural disaster or disease outbreak or war that occurs in this world, it is possible to be prepared. Moving forward, this preparedness must include people living with disabilities. Perhaps one day world leaders will come to the realization that the unique experiences of those who have disabilities are not inconveniences or burdens, but rather, a flavourful cocktail of new perspectives and ideas to bring forward.

References

Battle, D. E. (2014). Persons with communication disabilities in natural disasters, war, and/or conflict. Communication Disorders Quarterly, 36(4), 231–240. https://doi.org/10.1177/1525740114545980

Centers for Disease Control and Prevention. (2022, October 28). Disability impacts all of us infographic. Centers for Disease Control and Prevention. Retrieved December 9, 2022, from https://www.cdc.gov/ncbddd/disabilityandhealth/infographic-disability-impacts-all.html#:~:text=26%20percent%20

Lund, E. M., & Ayers, K. B. (2022). Ever-changing but always constant: "waves" of disability discrimination during the COVID-19 pandemic in the United States. Disability and Health Journal, 15(4), 101374. https://doi.org/10.1016/j.dhjo.2022.101374

Mewes, R., Rief, W., Stenzel, N., Glaesmer, H., Martin, A., & Brahler, E. (2009). Answer to the comment on: What is "normal" disability? an investigation of disability in the general population. Pain, 144(3), 342. https://doi.org/10.1016/j.pain.2009.05.011

Morris, S., Fawcett, G., Brisebois, L., & Hughes, J. (2018, November 28). A demographic, employment and income profile of Canadians with disabilities aged 15 years and over, 2017. Retrieved December 9, 2022, from https://www150.statcan.gc.ca/n1/pub/89-654-x/89-654-x2018002-eng.htm

Nedha. (2015, June 22). Difference between equity and Equality. Compare the Difference Between Similar Terms. Retrieved December 9, 2022, from https://www.differencebetween.com/difference-between-equity-and-vs-equality/

Penrose, W. D. (2015). The discourse of disability in Ancient Greece. Classical World, 108(4), 499–523. https://doi.org/10.1353/clw.2015.0068

Phillips, A. (2022, November 18). We're all implicated in Michael Fraser's decision to die. thestar.com. Retrieved December 9, 2022, from https://www.thestar.com/opinion/star-columnists/2022/11/18/were-all-implicated-in-michael-frasers-decision-to-die.html

Public Service Alliance of Canada [PSAC]. (n.d.). Pandemic is increasing inequality for people with disabilities. PSAC. Retrieved December 9, 2022, from https://psacunion.ca/international-day-of-persons-with-disabilities

Rotarou, E. S., Sakellariou, D., Kakoullis, E. J., & Warren, N. (2021). Disabled people in the time of COVID-19: Identifying needs, promoting inclusivity. Journal of Global Health, 11. https://doi.org/10.7189/jogh.11.03007

Tooley, M. (1972). Abortion and Infanticide. Philosophy & Public Affairs, 2(1), 37–65. http://www.jstor.org/stable/2264919

Utz, S. W. (1999). Enabling america: Assessing the role of Rehabilitation Science and Engineering. Family & Community Health, 22(2), 97–98. https://doi.org/10.1097/00003727-199907000-00011

Vera Kubenz Research Fellow – GCRF Network+ "Disability Under Siege." (2022, September 13). Disabled people are being left out of COVID recovery. here are five ways to change that. The Conversation. Retrieved December 9, 2022, from https://theconversation.com/disabled-people-are-being-left-out-of-covid-recovery-here-are-five-ways-to-change-that-181362

Chapter 5
The polarizing effects of the COVID-19 pandemic within the business world

By Ameer Hasan

Introduction

Before the beginning of 2020 the name COVID-19 held no significance to it. Nearly 3 years later, there's not a single individual that has not been affected by it. Covid impacted the world in a significant way. Although there are no longer lockdowns in effect, many other aspects are still felt to this day. Many essentials such as the price of both refined and unrefined fuels are intertwined with the transport of many goods and therefore prices of things such as groceries and other essentials have been inflated. Although many people think due to this inflation all businesses are profiting that is not the case. Big conglomerates who rule their respective markets do. Not the small businesses. The scary part is that small businesses make up 98% of businesses in Canada (Sood et al., 2021). Regardless of the percentage of businesses that are small they are still surviving meaning that businesses have shifted to a model that allowed them to survive COVID and thrive in the world after it is gone.

Adapting to a New World: Online Sales

The COVID-19 pandemic has allowed businesses to adapt a new model that includes low overhead while still maintaining the same pricing allowing for possible increase in profits. They are doing this by putting up barriers, having mask mandates, reducing operating hours, applying for government aid, letting go a substantial amount of employees and continuing business online (Sood et al., 2021). This online sales model has helped a lot of Canadian businesses keep their doors open. In 2019 17.9% of total sales amongst all companies in Canada were made online. These pre-pandemic numbers were improved in 2020 as online sales increased an impressive 4% to bring the total online purchases to 21.6% (Sood et al., 2021). Statistics show that around one third (30.4%) of small business owners expected covid to affect their business in a negative way causing a loss in sales. On the other side of the spectrum only 19.2% of bigger businesses (upwards of 100 employees) also reported that they expected a loss in sales. A loss in sales and revenue was expected across the board. Looking at the numbers reported by Stat Canada it shows that 42.3% of businesses sales remained around the same and relatively unaffected by the pandemic. While 41.8% of businesses saw a decrease in business. The remaining percentage lies in the 8.3% of companies that actually saw an increase in business, and the remaining 7.3% was not eligible to be a part of the statistic (Sood et al., 2021). In 2019 Canada's total onlines sales was sitting at 35.79 billion dollars in revenue. While this sounds like an astronomical amount of onlines sales COVID caused it to increase exponentially. In 2020 online sales increased to 46.09 billion dollars in revenue. 2020 was the year of COVID and as previously stated this allowed for a new market to emerge and become the new normal. The following 2 years both increased to 58.01 and 66.92 billion dollars in revenue respectively in 2021 and 2022. This exponential growth is projected to continue for the foreseeable future, with the next 3 years predicted to have 77.39, 89.45, and 103.6 billion dollars in projected revenue for online sales in Canada (Stipp, 2022). This was another example of how much COVID has changed the entire outlook of the business world. However because of this, a new era of business has been launched into the foreground and it is increasing in popularity with each passing year. Everything from buying underwear to getting groceries has become digitized even a lot of healthcare is digitized in this new online centric world.

Pandemic Conceived Government Aid

While businesses in Canada were adapting to the new world over 5800 businesses were part of a survey taken stateside. This study was to see the effects of COVID-19 on small businesses from March 28th to April 4th 2020. There were many different themes and common recurrences. One of those was employees getting laid off, this had happened mere weeks into the first lockdown. Another thing that they found was business owners had varying ideas regarding the length of the closures and their overall effect on business. Another alarming reality is how financially fragile many small businesses really are. 2 weeks of cash on hand was all the median of businesses had, those of which had approximately $10,000 in monthly expenses (Bartik et al., 2020). The impact of COVID-19 was felt on a global scale, nevertheless every country reacted differently. However in this aspect of it there are many similarities between the way it affected small Canadian businesses along with small American businesses. Something that the United States has is the CARES act program. The Coronavirus Aid, Relief, and Economic Security or more commonly referred to as CARES is an act passed by the United States congress which provides Americans financial assistance. This act was passed on the 25th of March and 2 days later the law was put into effect (U.S Department of Treasury, 2021). CARES covered rent, payroll, lease, utility, and mortgage payment for the first 8 weeks after the act was passed. To actually get the money reimbursed there was a requirement that at least 75% of the loan was used on payroll. The amount varied based on the amount required for the stated variables (Bartik et al., 2020). CARES is also more of a grant than a loan as the government was trying to help their citizens without knowing the duration of the pandemic, leading to them not making it into a loan so much as a grant. Similarly Canada had their CERB program. Canadians who were at least 15 years old and had lost their income due to COVID-19 were given money. To be eligible for it Canadians were required to not have made over $1000 via employment or self employment for 14 or more consecutive days within the 4 week CERB period (Service Canada, 2022). Overall government assistance was an integral part of the COVID-19 r elief effort.

Companies First Response To COVID-19

Being the first to a movement could be beneficial or detrimental to a company who issues a statement or offers a service regarding any particular relevant event. The first companies that responded to the COVID-19 pandemic ended up issuing public statements regarding the pandemic. Others gave up their assembly line to produce personal protective equipment (PPE) to combat the spread of the virus (Dreier & Nelson, 2020). From others contributing to funding covid related research, many different companies found many different ways to aid in the fight against the pandemic. Through the means of research, government aid, and partnering with nonprofit organizations. The influence of these actions allowed for the pandemic to be handled better than expected. As unity was a common theme throughout. TikTok is an app which millions of people used during the pandemic. A sort of community formed on there, where everyone used eachother as a support to help cope with the pandemic. Businesses alike also migrated to TikTok to stay relevant during the multiple lockdowns, companies such as DuoLingo made funny and shareable content which both highlighted their services and took people's mind away from everything happening in the world. Many different businesses took off because of the app, leading it to become a new marketing tool for businesses. Instagram, Snapchat, and TikTok are now the major ways for businesses to market themselves amongst this new wave of social media consumption. Regardless of the company and what platform (their own or social media such as TikTok) they used, these companies had to be innovative to get their message across. For these companies to be the first responders to something as devastating as this pandemic, they needed to have certain traits such as, leaders that were brand conscious, individuals who were not afraid of innovation, and collaborators who were well-networked (Dreier & Nelson, 2020). Many very large and relatively small companies alike gave back during the pandemic as previously mentioned, with the larger ones making monetary contributions and the smaller ones offering whatever they could every business needed to maintain their public relations and public perception during the pandemic to help stay afloat. Circling back to TikTok's place in the first response to COVID, many brands had to find ways to appeal to the apps algorithm, this would require more relatable and broad hashtags and topics as everyones for you page (FYP) is tailored to them. As everyone's FYP was quite different, these marketing teams had to do extensive market research and try new ideas to appear on more devices and different kinds of peoples feeds, giving more exposure to the company and product. The businesses that built well networked connections ended up inheriting a plethora of different advantages. These could have been things such as: having the upper hand in the business relationship or being giving back to the community. The upper hand is had with a good business relationship as this can bring an extra bargaining chip into deal. An example of this is Salesforce leveraging their connections in a deal with Alibaba in 2020 for 50 million pieces of PPE. Their relationship with Walmart, Fedex, Gap, Uber and others helped close the deal with Alibaba (Dreier & Nelson, 2020).

Building Businesses Post Pandemic

Technically we are still in the pandemic with COVID hiding in the shadows, but for the most part the world has moved on. Businesses have opened their doors, schools are back to in person attendance, and lockdowns are a thing of the past. It is easy to get lost in the sheer carnage that the pandemic brought in its wake, but for the betterment of the economy it is smarter to look forward and try to figure out methods to move on. It was reported that in the United Kingdom the number of new business registrations started increasing. Meanwhile the freelancing service Fiverr saw an increase of around 77% of earnings in 2020 (Aslam, 2021). This is due to the increase in unemployment and people trying to find alternative methods of earning money. Just like this COVID previous pandemics resulted in a shift in the market with different businesses emerging from the rubble. In 1918 the flu pandemic led to the explosion and was the catalyst of the explosion of the stock market. After this global pandemic things such as digital payments, remote working, robotics, and healthtech have really emerged as large parts of the economy. Evolution through means of destruction has been historically proven to occur plenty of times. Harvard Business Review states that in order to start and/or maintain a successful business in this new world post pandemic, 2 things must be had. A carefully chosen sustainable business plan that will be pandemic/recession proof, and a crafted business plan to hold the market (Byrnes & Wass, 2021). It has been discussed that a majority of companies actually have not come to terms that this is the new reality in a post pandemic era. This is due to the fact that most companies executives run up the ranks with their tried and true methods of the past, in this new digital era none of those methods are effective anymore (Byrnes & Wass, 2021). To truly adapt and survive in this market there's only two paths; the current executives can get out of their comfort zones and attempt new strategies, or they can be replaced entirely with new and younger individuals who understand what it takes to succeed in today's digital world.

A Helping Hand: How Corporations Help Support The Future

The future can be a very exciting and terrifying thing all at once, the future in a COVID free world and navigating a business through it is no simple thing. As previously mentioned the whole play book has to be thrown out in favor of a new more modern and digital approach. This is all relatively uncharted for most businesses as corporations such as Facebook and Amazon both have been giants in the digital realm, their recent growth despite already being multi billion dollar companies shows how COVID has changed the landscape of the business world as a whole. Zoom, a name in which no one had heard of before COVID, is now a multi billion dollar corporation (Macrotrend, 2022). This just shows how although COVID took many jobs and lives it is not necessarily a bad thing. There is a positive side or any negative situation. The world is going to learn from these past two years and it is gonna move on and keep everything in mind so that if anything similar to this happens in the future, governments and businesses know what to do to keep the catastrophic results to a minimum. Companies such as Google have started to offer programs for free that allow individuals to earn certifications in certain fields like: project management, IT, e-commerce, and digital marketing (Google, 2022). This can help land a job after completing the courses or allow the individual to start their own business with their new qualifications. How some companies have responded to the pandemic lending a helping hand to those who needed it. This concept is reminiscent of the well known quote; "Give a man a fish, and you feed him for a day. Teach a man to fish, and you feed him for a lifetime." In this case the ability to fish is teaching a skill that results in a certification that can help land a job or start a company keeping the individual afloat. Another example of this is when the initial lockdown hit and many companies were not able to pay their employees, Microsoft continued their payroll for the hourly workers on the campus regardless of reduced hours or not (Hyder, 2021). This likely prevented their workers from running into a plethora of different financial challenges and woes, like many other people due to the pandemic. Video sharing service Loom also made their pro version free for teachers and students in 2020, while slashing their price in half for others in the process. This was beneficial as everyone was online for school and work. The schools didn't have to drain their funding just to deliver remote classes and businesses got a 50% discount which would not have hurt them as much with the whole world in a pandemic. While also helping others out Loom ended up increasing the desirability of their product hence leading to an increase in sales. Even with offering plans for free and half off Looms revenue went from a measly $750,000 in 2019 to a whopping $10,000,000 a year later (Khemchandani, 2022). Furthermore in the following year of 2021 Looms revenue more than tripled at 35 million dollars . Loom's decision to help others out during COVID ultimately led to a situation where everyone involved benefitted. A more business oriented relief was a summit called "Business Resilience: Thriving in Crucial Times" offered by Forbes8 on the 20th of March 2020. This event goes over how businesses can survive through COVID. Many best selling authors such as Rohit Bhargava and Chris Brogan were featured at the event which many had canceled on due to the pandemic (Morgan, 2021). The fact that these companies are even doing things that benefit others shows that investing in future means that everyone has to come together and share knowledge and skills otherwise society would not be able move forward alone, J.K Rowling famously said "We are only as strong as we are united, as weak as we are divided". These companies prove how accurate this quote is as their outreach has promoted unity. A company that has done exceptionally well due to COVID is Amazon, when the initial influx of business came towards Amazon they started giving out raises and hired 100,000 more employees (Morgan, 2021). While this was before their controversy surrounding the warehouses and mistreatment of employees the idea was still a very constructive one at the time. COVID rocked businesses in industries that were nowhere near as volatile as the restaurant industry, in wake of that UberEats and Doordash both waived commission fees for their independent partners. This means all the small asd independent restaurants that are not huge chains or franchises do not have to pay the delivery services a percentage of their earnings, keeping all revenue to themselves in a time where restaurants took a major hit. COVID research needed all the funding it could get, Dolce & Gabbana ended up joining forces with Humanitas University to help fund COVID research (Morgan, 2021). Having a fashion and multimillion dollar giant such as Dolce & Gabbana use their money to help the funding towards covid research showed customers that this business cares about problems bigger than just their own sales.

Conclusion

The polarizing effects of the COVID-19 pandemic within the business world were: adapting to a new world with online sales, the pandemic conceived government aid, how companies first responded to COVID, building businesses post pandemic, and how corporations helped support the future. With onlines sales taking the reins as a juggernaut in the future of sales in Canada and exponentially growing it truly is the new normal for businesses. With aid to both businesses and citizens alike COVID forced the government to help out their countries and they stepped up and had plans in place for everyone. That being said, all the government aid companies had to react to the first effects of COVID with statements released to the press and partnerships with nonprofits to help others during COVID all while adapting the way they do business. With sustainable business plans for building businesses in the future and companies lowering or even entirely removing their prices when helping out during COVID. Everyone did their part and it shows how the business world has changed due to this virus. All in all with all the statistics and new business plans and marketing approaches the entire world has changed for the better or the worst because of the COVID-19 pandemic.

References

Aslam, S. (2021, June 17). Council post: Three tips for starting a business after the pandemic. Forbes. Retrieved November 24, 2022, from https://www.forbes.com/sites/forbesbusinesscouncil/2021/06/17/three-tips-for-starting-a-business-after-the-pandemic/?sh=dd5219b31d15

Bartik, A. W., Bertrand, M., Cullen, Z., Glaeser, E. L., & Luca, M. (2020, July 10). The impact of covid-19 on small business outcomes and ... - PNAS. The impact of COVID-19 on small business outcomes and expectations. Retrieved November 21, 2022, from https://www.pnas.org/doi/10.1073/pnas.2006991117

Byrnes, J., & Wass, J. (2021, May 3). How to create a winning post-pandemic business model. Harvard Business Review. Retrieved November 25, 2022, from https://hbr.org/2021/03/how-to-create-a-winning-post-pandemic-business-model

Dreier, L., & Nelson, J. (2020, July 6). Why some companies leapt to support the COVID-19 response. World Economic Forum. Retrieved December 4, 2022, from https://www.weforum.org/agenda/2020/07/companies-action-support-covid-19-response/

Google. (n.d.). Job-ready skills you can put to work. Online Courses with Certificates - Grow with Google. Retrieved November 25, 2022, from https://grow.google/certificates/?utm_source=gDigital&utm_medium=paidha&utm_campaign=can-sem-bk-gen-exa-glp-br&utmcontent=keyword&gclid=CjwKCAiA7IGcBhA8EiwAFfUDsVAeHOq6a19UIpA2Pk2W9RRGA3Qy2m7ame5iPtDNC_aHW74qrRmdFBoClXAQAvD_BwE#?modal_active=none

Hyder, S. (2021, August 23). Coronavirus Champions: A running list of brands getting it right. Forbes. Retrieved December 4, 2022, from https://www.forbes.com/sites/shamahyder/2020/03/15/coronavirus-champions-a-running-list-of-brands-getting-it-right/?sh=24ca77215815

Khemchandani, M. (2022, October 22). 10 loom user and Company Facts and Statistics (2022). MK's Guide. Retrieved December 4, 2022, from https://www.mksguide.com/loom-user-statistics/#:~:text=Loom's%20total%20revenue%20in%202021,in%202019%20was%20about%20%24750%2C000.

MacroTrends. (2022, January 1). Zoom Video Communications Net Worth 2019-2022: ZM. Macrotrends. Retrieved November 25, 2022, from https://www.macrotrends.net/stocks/charts/ZM/zoom-video-communications/net-worth#:~:text=How%20much%20a%20company%20is,24%2C%202022%20is%20%2422.66B.

Morgan, B. (2021, December 10). 50 ways companies are giving back during the coronavirus pandemic. Forbes. Retrieved December 4, 2022, from https://www.forbes.com/sites/blakemorgan/2020/03/17/50-ways-companies-are-giving-back-during-the-corona-pandemic/?sh=38e4b1074723

Service Canada. (2022, August 3). Government of Canada. Canada Emergency Response Benefit (CERB) - Canada.ca. Retrieved November 21, 2022, from https://www.canada.ca/en/services/benefits/ei/cerb-application.html#h2.03

Sood, S., Tam, S., & Johnston, C. (2021, March 10). Impact of COVID-19 on small businesses in Canada, irst quarter of 2021. Retrieved November 22, 2022, from https://www150.statcan.gc.ca/n1/pub/45-28-0001/2021001/article/00009-eng.htm

Stipp, H. (2022, October 21). Canada: Retail e-commerce revenue 2025. Statista. Retrieved December 4, 2022, from https://www.statista.com/statistics/289741/canada-retail-e-commerce-sales/

U.S Department of Treasury. (2021, April 13). About the cares act and the consolidated appropriations act. U.S. Department of the Treasury. Retrieved November 23, 2022, from https://home.treasury.gov/policy-issues/coronavirus/about-the-cares-act

Chapter 6
Effects of the COVID-19 pandemic on depression and mental health

By Jaelyn Kupilik

Introduction

The Coronavirus Infectious Disease 2019 (COVID-19) pandemic created an inundation of illness, mortality, and isolation worldwide. Society experienced lasting effects, and in concurrence, billions of people's lives were altered. Due to the efforts of governments and the World Health Organization (WHO), lockdowns and safety protocols were implemented worldwide, pushing people inside their homes away from loved ones, friends, and the workplace. The safety protocols and isolation constructed both a lack of human interaction and increased stress. Two factors may enable symptoms of depression or anxiety, as seen through the studies completed post-pandemic. An area of concern for researchers in psychology relates to the possible effects of the pandemic on mental illness. Multiple studies research the effect the pandemic had on rates of stress, depression, anxiety, and suicide.

Since the outbreak of COVID-19 and the following lockdowns, depression and other mental illness has increased within the general population due to isolation and stress. Symptoms have correspondingly been shown to proliferate throughout the pandemic for individuals with pre-existing mental illnesses. COVID-19 detrimentally affected mental illness through social barriers and stress, significantly increasing depression and anxiety worldwide.

Coronavirus Infectious Disease 2019 (COVID-19): A Pandemic
COVID-19 is noted as an infectious disease that is caused by the SARS-CoV-2 virus. It was first reported and detected in Wuhan, China, on December 31, 2019. The disease quickly became prevalent

worldwide, infecting over 600 million individuals and causing 6 million deaths as of November 2020 (World Health Organization, 2020). Due to the spread of the disease, safety protocols were quickly implemented by various authorities worldwide; protocols included isolation, social distancing, curfews, and mask mandates. No visitors were allowed in hospitals, and temperature and symptom testing became prevalent in numerous health centers and hospitals. The sudden onset of COVID-19 and the implementation of life-changing protocols caused mass stress and hysteria. Many people were purchasing large quantities of food and house supplies, worried about lockdowns. COVID-19 symptoms include fever, shortness of breath, cough, chest pain, and loss of taste or smell (World Health Organization). The pandemic caused unfavorable outcomes for all individuals and altered the lives of millions; many individuals began working from home. For students, online learning became the primary mode of schooling. Individuals experienced increased mental health issues due to drastic lifestyle changes and social isolation. One prominent factor individuals faced was increased stress.

Stress and COVID-19

Stress is a biological, physiological response to a perceived threat. In theory, specific volumes of stress are observed as healthy, while an overabundance of stress may lead to adverse health outcomes. Barbosa-Camacho et al. 1 (2022) explicates that stress affects the prefrontal cortex, amygdala, and hippocampus. The neurological effects of stress affect how individuals process and retain information from the world. Stressors also weaken the immune system, increase the likelihood of infection, and psychologically affect individuals. An example is the aftermath of the SARS pandemic in 2003, where diagnoses of posttraumatic stress syndrome, depression, and anxiety increased (Barbosa-Camacho et al., 2022). Pandemics such as COVID-19 or SARS increase stressors within individuals' lives; some stressors may be related to finances, health, and family. Though various stressors are apparent in everyday life, the stress added from a pandemic creates lasting outcomes on physical and mental health. For example, increased stress can lead to depressive symptoms. An analysis by Gurshaan Bajaj et al. (2021) presents that 6.40% of internet users claimed to experience indicators of depression following the start of the pandemic. This percentage equates to 1,978 participants out of 30,892, where 28,915 were depressed prior to the pandemic (Bajaj et al., 2021). The data elucidate the hypothesis that depressive feelings increased during the COVID-19 pandemic. Though depression is not a direct outcome of stress, symptoms of depression can generate from high levels of stress over time. Stress is one factor of several that can cause depressive feelings in individuals.

Depressive Symptoms: Ties to the Pandemic

Depression is a common mood disorder that numerous individuals experience or suffer from in their lifetime. Depression's severity varies, and symptoms include temporary melancholy or an ongoing chemical imbalance. The common mood disorder can be due to stress, bereavement, or anxiety. Depression was a cause of worry for psychologists and psychiatrists during the pandemic due to increased stressors and isolating factors put on individuals. Joshi et al. (2022) state that during the pandemic, depression increased substantially. Factors of depression include increased fatigue, feelings of melancholy, and in severe cases, ideation of suicide (Zhou et al., 2021). Galea et al. (2020) explicate that the pandemic curated an influx of mental health issues to individuals worldwide and that these issues are pertinent in the long term. In other words, individuals who experience mental health issues due to the pandemic may continue to experience these symptoms.

A study completed by Zhou et al. (2021) researched the effect of the COVID-19 pandemic on depression in Australia. They used user-generated content on Twitter to assess depression in individuals residing in Australia, and the results showcased a strong correlation between depression and COVID-19 protocols implemented by the Australian government. Increases in depression occurred in four stages; after the outbreak of COVID-19, during increases in confirmed cases, the implementation of COVID-19 protocols, and the relaxation of these same protocols (Zhou et al., 2021). Questions concerning why depression rates increased during the relaxation of COVID-19 protocols include the theory that individuals' stress of infection and rising cases from increased human interaction was the leading cause of depression in Australians. Though the study focused on Australian data, many other countries likely experienced similar spikes in depression rates throughout the pandemic.

Ori et al. (2023) completed a longitudinal study in the Netherlands that looked at patterns of Major Depressive Disorder (MDD), Generalized Anxiety Disorder (GAD), and suicidal ideation in the population. Results support prior findings from other countries that during the lockdowns prevalence of MDD and GAD increased. Specifically, MDD and GAD increased substantially during the third lockdown in the Netherlands, which was characterized by strict measures implemented by the government (Ori et al., 2023). However, the data conveys that in-between periods of lockdowns. There were declines in rates of MDD and GAD, supporting the hypothesis that the lockdowns directly affected individuals' mental well-being (Ori et al., 2023).

The COVID-19 pandemic curated an influx of stress and anxiety for billions of individuals worldwide and significantly affected depression rates in Australia, the Netherlands, and likely in other countries. The long-term effects of these rates of depression and GAD have not been concluded yet; however, individuals can expect that depression rates may increase over time due to the lasting effects of the pandemic. The studies' results depict a clear pattern that lockdowns caused a statistically significant increase in the prevalence of depression and GAD. Increases in mental health disorders are detrimental to the overall health and well-being of the population.

Anxiety

Anxiety may be a normal and healthy coping mechanism for a perceived threat. However, severe anxiety can cause poor health outcomes, a weakened immune system, and difficulty in life. Due to COVID-19, many individuals experienced increased anxiety about their health and the health of their loved ones. Researchers worry that with increased stress from the pandemic, an individual's likelihood of drug and substance abuse may also increase. Anxiety symptoms can range in severity, and the source of the anxiety can also alter. Individuals may experience anxiety concerning their health, or they may experience anxiety towards social situations. Severe symptoms may be debilitating to individuals and the ones around them.

Nonetheless, anxiety is a healthy physiological reaction when in moderation. A study by Lee et al. (2020) looks at fear and anxiety concerning COVID-19. Researchers used the Coronavirus Anxiety Scale (CAS) to assess participants' anxiety levels towards the pandemic. Results show that participants previously diagnosed with COVID-19 received higher scores on the CAS. Additionally, individuals with a history of anxiety also had higher CAS scores (Lee et al., 2020). Higher CAS scores were positively correlated with worry about COVID-19, substance abuse, hopelessness, and past suicidal ideation (Lee et al., 2020). The Lee et al. (2020) study signifies that the pandemic caused significant anxiety in individuals. Though the study was focused on U.S. citizens, individuals from other countries likely experienced similar symptoms concerning the pandemic.

Prior to the pandemic, anxiety and depression were leading disorders in the world (Santomauro et al., 2021). Millions of individuals suffer from the symptoms of anxiety and depression. However, with the life-changing effects of the pandemic, many wonder about the correlation between COVID-19 and mental health rates. In a study completed by Santomauro et al., 2021, results display a positive correlation between mental illness and SARS-CoV-2 infection rates. In other words, as confirmed cases of COVID-19 increased, so did the rates of depression and anxiety. A possible explanation for these trends is the effect of sudden life changes on individuals. Many individuals may be unable to adapt as effectively as others in unknown situations, leading to substantial mental health issues.

In some cases, depression and anxiety can lead to suicidal ideation. In Japan, data displays that from February to June 2020, suicide rates decreased substantially. However, the suicide rates increased by 16% later that year. The initial decline seen after a societal shock is called the pulling-together effect or the honey money phase. During this phase, individuals work together to achieve communal good; individuals express feelings of hope and motivation.

Consequently, following the honeymoon phase is the disillusionment phase, including feelings of disappointment and distress (Kõlves et al., 2013). The time of the honeymoon phase is thought to be the reason behind decreased suicide rates after societal shock, and the disillusionment phase is often described with increases in mental health issues and suicidal ideation. Therefore, the increase in suicide rates in Japan may be related to the disillusionment phase of behavioural and psychological responses to natural disasters (Kõlves et al., 2013). In all, stress significantly increased throughout the pandemic.

Effects of COVID-19 on Individuals with Previously Diagnosed Mental Health Disorders

Studies concerning the effect of the pandemic on individuals' mental health explicate an increase in mental health issues. However, not many studies discuss the pandemic's impact on individuals with previously diagnosed mental disorders. A cross-sectional study by Campos et al. (2022) discusses the theory that individuals with a pre-existing mental disorder had lasting impacts due to COVID-19. Restriction, isolation, and changes in lifestyle due to the pandemic can all impact an individual's mental health. However, individuals with pre-existing mental disorders may be more susceptible to harmful impacts. 31% of participants in the study indicated that they had experienced a mental health disorder at some point in their life prior to the COVID-19 pandemic (Campos et al., 2022). Mental disorders reported in Campos et al. (2022) study include anxiety, depression, bipolar disorder, and panic disorder. Comorbidities between disorders were also included in the study. The study's results indicate that participants with pre-existing mental disorders were significantly more susceptible to psychological impacts due to the pandemic (Campos et al., 2022).

Additionally, individuals with bipolar disorder or combined disorder had an increased likelihood of experiencing psychological impacts (Campos et al., 2022). The study's results are concerning due to the increasing percentage of mental disorders worldwide. Campos et al. (2022) additionally state that individuals with pre-existing disorders are less likely to receive mental health care than those without a disorder. Lack of mental health support mixed with life-changing events in individuals with pre-existing mental disorders may decrease overall well-being, causing individuals to worsen their symptoms. Without proper support, individuals may seek substances or drugs to aid their declining well-being, causing increased addictions and overdoses in Canada.

In addition to the results found in Campos et al. (2022) study, data illustrates that females and youth are in the high-risk category for psychological implications due to the pandemic. A possible explanation is that younger individuals have less developed coping and behavioural mechanisms, which leads to increased psychological implications (Campos et al., 2022). Regarding sex differences in the study, women often internalize issues and stress compared to men (Campos et al., 2022). Another possible explanation for the data explicates that due to societal influences, men may not report their issues as often as women or youth do because of the stigma surrounding men and emotions (Campos et al., 2022). Though all individuals are at risk of facing changes in mental health throughout their lifetime, Campos et al. (2022) study illustrates that those with pre-existing mental disorders are at high risk of psychological implications during the pandemic, particularly youth and women.

Suicide and Suicidal Ideation: COVID-19

In recent times, the rate of suicide has been increasing worldwide. The increasing depression and anxiety rates throughout the pandemic create concern about the prevalence of suicide. Before the pandemic, individuals between the ages of 15 to 30 years old were considered at the highest risk for suicide and suicidal ideation (Berisa et al., 2022). The World Health Organization (WHO) states that over 700,000 individuals die from suicide yearly, with 77% being from low- and middle-income countries. For every suicide, there are more than 20 suicide attempts (Berisa et al., 2022). Data shows that there is an apparent epidemic in the world, with increasing suicide rates every year and a high prevalence of suicidal ideation; governments must find a way to aid in the mental well-being of citizens. Following the decrease in COVID-19, various researchers have studied the relationship between the pandemic and suicide, or suicidal ideation. Though one may hypothesize an influx in suicide rates during the pandemic, studies found that the rate of suicide decreased or remained stable. Berisa et al. (2022) looked at patterns of suicide among youth during the pandemic and found a non-significant increase in suicide during the lockdowns. Another study completed by Antonova et al. (2022) supports the findings that in comparison to years prior to COVID-19, suicide rates remain the same. However, Antonova et al. (2022) explicate that the findings may be unreliable due to the lack of data regarding suicide rates.

Suicidal ideation is described as thoughts of death and self-harm. Suicidal ideations have been linked to various mental disorders, such as MDD, bipolar personality disorder, and GAD. In addition to suicide rates during COVID-19, researchers have studied the relationship between suicidal ideation and the pandemic. Bismark et al. (2022) studied Australian healthcare workers and suicidal ideation throughout COVID-19. Results illustrate that 10.5%, or 1 in 10 healthcare workers, experienced suicidal ideation or self-harm thoughts.

Additionally, individuals were more likely to experience suicidal ideation if they had friends or family members infected with COVID-19, were living alone, were male, had prior mental illness, and had a history of alcohol abuse (Bismark et al., 2022). In another study on suicidal ideation during the pandemic, results state a statistically significant increase in suicidal ideation, particularly for younger individuals (Gelezelyte et al., 2022). Suicidal ideation has been linked to an increased prevalence of depression, anxiety, posttraumatic stress disorder, and burnout compared to individuals with no reports of suicidal ideation (Bismark et al., 2022). In conjunction with the results found for individuals with pre-existing mental disorders, individuals who were younger or had prior mental health concerns were less likely to seek support when experiencing suicidal ideation or thoughts of self-harm (Bismark et al., 2022). The results are concerning because those who seemingly need mental health support the most are not receiving it. Multiple factors may play a role in the reasoning for this occurrence. For instance, individuals may not have received proper support in past experiences or may not know about support systems available in their country. Nonetheless, it is essential that the government implements appropriate aid and care for individuals experiencing suicidal ideation. Without proper care, the overall well-being of individuals will be at risk.

Conclusion

The COVID-19 pandemic brought on many changes in society, particularly in how individuals live their lives. The vast majority of the population was forced inside their homes for months, creating a lack of human connection for millions. Fear also spread with an unknown infectious disease spreading quickly around the globe. Many individuals could not say goodbye to their friends or loved ones and were left with depression or anxiety. The studies discussed above examine how the pandemic affects the mental health of the world population. Depression, anxiety, stress, suicide, and suicidal ideation are all factors concerning psychologists. The pandemic created extraneous stress in individuals' lives due to restrictions placed by the government and the inability to complete normal daily activities. Stress is known to cause depressive symptoms in specific individuals potentially, and with the increase in stress, researchers additionally saw an increase in depression, particularly during the phases of lockdowns (Ori et al., 2023). Anxiety was also hypothesized to increase during the pandemic. This was likely due to the lack of information available to the general public.

The prevalence of anxiety showed similarities to the patterns of depression during COVID-19, where spikes occurred during the lockdowns (Kõlves et al., 2013).

The effects of the pandemic on individuals with pre-existing mental disorders were additionally studied, and results indicated that individuals with pre-existing mental disorders were more susceptible to psychological impacts from the pandemic (Campos et al., 2022). The results also stated that individuals with pre-existing disorders were less likely to seek support in comparison to their counterparts (Campos et al., 2022). Lastly, suicide and suicidal ideation was additional factor that was researched. In opposition to depression and anxiety, suicide rates decreased or remained stable during COVID-19 (Berisa et al., 2022). Conversely, there is little information or data about suicide rates during the pandemic. Thus, the results may be unreliable. On the other hand, suicidal ideation tended to increase during the pandemic, particularly for healthcare workers and younger individuals (Bismark et al., 2022).

In conclusion, the pandemic significantly affects the mental well-being of individuals worldwide. Though suicide rates remained stable, rates of depression, anxiety, and suicidal ideation displayed statistically significant increases. The mental well-being of individuals was substantially affected throughout the pandemic. Further research must be done to come to a reliable conclusion, specifically longitudinal designs that may be able to identify patterns of depression and other mental illness throughout the pandemic. Nonetheless, the data present conveys an understanding that mental well-being is a crucial, yet often overlooked, aspect in the existence of humanity.

References

Antonova, H., Pamidimukkala, E. C. S., Liao, S., & Ceesay, E. (2022). Suicide Rate and Factors Analysis: Pre and Post COVID Pandemic Data Analysis. 2022 IEEE International IOT, Electronics and Mechatronics Conference (IEMTRONICS), 1–8. https://doi.org/10.1109/IEMTRONICS55184.2022.9795714

Bajaj, G. S., Yadav, H., Sahdev, H. S., Sah, S., & Kaur, P. (2021). Mental health analysis during COVID-19: A comparison before and during the pandemic. 2021 IEEE 4th International Conference on Computing, Power, and Communication Technologies (GUCON)), 2021 IEEE 4th International Conference On, 1–7. https://doi.org/10.1109/GUCON50781.2021.9573763

Barbosa-Camacho et al. (2022). Depression, anxiety, and academic performance in COVID-19: a cross-sectional study. BMC Psychiatry, https://doi.org/10.1186/s12888-022-04062-3

Bersia, M., Koumantakis, E., Berchialla, P., Charrier, L., Ricotti, A., Grimaldi, P., Dalmasso, P., & Comoretto, R. I. (2022). Suicide spectrum among young people during the COVID-19 pandemic: A systematic review and meta-analysis. EClinicalMedicine, 54, 101705. https://doi.org/10.1016/j.eclinm.2022.101705

Bismark, M., Scurrah, K., Pascoe, A., Willis, K., Jain, R., & Smallwood, N. (2022). Thoughts of suicide or self-harm among Australian healthcare workers during the COVID-19 pandemic. Australian & New Zealand Journal of Psychiatry, 56(12), 1555–1565. https://doi.org/10.1177/00048674221075540

Campos, J. A. D. B., Campos, L. A., Martins, B. G., Valadão Dias, F., Ruano, R., & Maroco, J. (2022). The Psychological Impact of COVID-19 on Individuals With and Without Mental Health Disorders. Psychological Reports, 125(5), 2435–2455. https://doi.org/10.1177/00332941211026850

Galea S, Merchant RM, Lurie N. The Mental Health Consequences of COVID-19 and Physical Distancing: The Need for Prevention and Early Intervention. JAMA Intern Med. 2020;180(6):817–818. https://doi:10.1001/jamainternmed.2020.1562

Gelezelyte, O., Kazlauskas, E., Brailovskaia, J., Margraf, J., & Truskauskaite-Kuneviciene, I. (2022). Suicidal ideation in university students in Lithuania amid the COVID-19 pandemic: A prospective study with pre-pandemic measures. Death Studies, 46(10), 2395–2403. https://doi.org/10.1080/07481187.2021.1947417

Kõlves, K., Kõlves, K. E., & De Leo, D. (2013). Natural disasters and suicidal behaviours: A systematic literature review. Journal of Affective Disorders, 146(1), 1–14. https://doi.org/10.1016/j.jad.2012.07.037

Lee, S. A. et al. (2020). Clinically Significant fear and anxiety of COVID-19: A psychometric examination of the Coronavirus Anxiety Scale. Psychiatry Research, vol 290 https://doi.org/10.1016/j.psychres.2020.113112

Lewis, K. J. S., Lewis, C., Roberts, A., Richards, N. A., Evison, C., Pearce, H. A., Lloyd, K., Meudell, A., Edwards, B. M., Robinson, C. A., Poole, R., John, A., Bisson, J. I., & Jones, I. (2022). The effect of the COVID-19 pandemic on mental health in individuals with pre-existing mental illness. BJPsych Open, 8. https://doi.org/10.1192/bjo.2022.25

Ori, A. P. S., Wieling, M., & van Loo, H. M. (2023). Longitudinal analyses of depression, anxiety, and suicidal ideation highlight greater prevalence in the northern Dutch population during the COVID-19 lockdowns. Journal of Affective Disorders, 323, 62–70. https://doi.org/10.1016/j.jad.2022.11.040

Santomauro, D. F., et al. (2021). Global prevalence and burden of depressive and anxiety disorders in 204 countries and territories in 2020 due to the COVID-19 pandemic. The Lancet, 398(10312), 1700–1712. https://doi.org/10.1016/S0140-6736(21)02143-7

Tanaka, T., & Okamoto, S. (2021). Increase in suicide following an initial decline during the COVID-19 pandemic in Japan. Nature Human Behaviour, 5(2), 229–238. https://doi.org/10.1038/s41562-020-01042-z

World Health Organization. (2020). COVID-19. https://www.who.int/health-topics/coronavirus#tab=tab_3

World Health Organization. (2021). Suicide. https://www.who.int/news-room/fact-sheets/detail/suicide

Chapter 7
Impact of COVID-19 on water and energy sector

By Ivy Truong

Water and sanitation

From decades of knowledge surrounding bacteria and viruses, handwashing has been the most basic frontline defense against mild and lethal diseases — ranging from a mild flu to cholera. This principle remains the same for COVID-19. However, a quarter of the world's population lacks access to a reliable supply of water and more than half of the world population lacks access to safe and maintained sanitation facilities. Even further, 22% of healthcare facilities in the least-developed countries lack access to clean water and reliable sanitation services (Butler et al., 2021). This makes something as simple as handwashing, near impossible. In the face of COVID-19, the inability to perform hygiene makes it difficult to curb the disease in these regions — exacerbating the decades-long water and sanitation crisis plaguing these countries. Prior to COVID-19, the global water sector was impacted by five major trends: global warming, increasing populations in areas with high water stress, rapid urbanization, the emergence of megacities, and aging infrastructure (Butler et al., 2021).

With the pandemic highlighting focused areas of concerns, further steps to address the neglected water sector were outlined. First, boosting water equity and affordability. As previously mentioned, the lack of clean water and reliable sanitation greatly amplified the impact of COVID-19 on those communities. Long-lasting solutions and improvements in the water sector directly personalized for the specific needs of each community is required. While temporary solutions such as water filters, temporary hand-washing stations, and external provision of water may help individuals in overcoming the current need for water, physical infrastructure needs should be addressed to provide a permanent solution for the entire community. This involves fixing leaking pipes, overwhelmed sewers, and outdated treatment plants (Ajami & Kane, 2020). Currently, the many regions of America and Canada face increasing lead exposure and contaminants that lower the drinking water equality and threaten the health of communities. Storm and wastewater presents a risk of water-borne infections when sewers are overwhelmed, overflowing onto streets and backyards.

Effects of COVID-19 on the energy sector

Lockdown procedures heavily restricted public movements, both domestically and internationally. The transportation sector is heavily dependent on the energy sector, and vice versa. With the sudden drop in travel, energy demands were greatly cut. This is further driven by the sudden transformation of work modality and lifestyle. Work-from-home, online schooling, and at-home entertainment altered energy consumption patterns from transportation-heavy to electricity use at home. Consequently, demand for transportation energy dropped while the demand for electric power rose significantly (Gollakota & Shu, 2022). Europe flights decreased by 89%, reducing consumption of airplane fuel (Nižetić, 2020) and motor travel decreased by 18.6% from 2019 to 2020, reducing consumption of motor gasoline (Zhang et al., 2021). The switch in energy demand was reflected in the price fluctuations; prices for gas and oil dropped while electrical rates increased. The disturbance in the energy equilibrium market created an energy war parallel to the prior War for Oil. Developed nations attempted to dominate and gain control of energy-rich countries.

Electricity consumption also realized a switch in usage patterns during the pandemic. Ultimately, electricity consumption in the residential sector was both directly and indirectly reduced by the pandemic. Shutdown of the industrial sector resulted in the reduction in total amount of electricity consumption. Lockdown policies also restricted social activities, indirectly reducing electricity consumption. Trends were also affected by COVID-19; there was a slight increase in overall residential electricity consumption throughout the day instead of being concentrated in the evening. There are three consumption patterns categorized under COVID-19 usage. First, due to the lockdown policy, remote work for students and adults increased residential electrical consumption in the daytime, as opposed to electricity usage at the workplace with less mobile device usage. Second, electricity consumption ordinarily ramps up in a narrow time frame in the morning due to work commuting and cooking breakfast, etc. During the pandemic, there was a much slower electricity consumption usage ramping up in the morning. Last, peak demand in the evening remained the same as pre-pandemic levels because consumption activities were less affected. TV-watching, preparing dinner, etc levels were sustained. Thus, the change in resident lifestyle and mode of work was reflected in the changes of electricity consumption patterns.

Climate impacts of COVID-19 caused by change in energy consumption.

While the significant decline in energy consumption and demand posed large problems to those sectors and economically, the significant reduction in fossil fuel combustion led to diminished greenhouse gas and air pollutant emissions. This was noticeable in highly developed regions primarily emitting sulfur dioxide and nitrogen dioxide, especially in the improvement of air quality. In a short amount of time, the effects of the accidental climate actions were noticed, generating hope and the possibility of taking steps towards climate change. The drastic change can be attributed to the degree of urbanization, amount of vehicle usage, and population density. Ultimately, this generated attraction towards improving air quality by focusing on the emission of air pollutants — nitrogen dioxide, ozone, carbon monoxide, sulfur dioxide and particulate matter.

Due to the lack of fossil fuel usage, nitrogen dioxide generated by fossil fuel combustion experienced a sharp decline (Chakraborty et al., 2020). The shutdown of power plants and coal mining also led to less burning of fossil fuels containing sulfur, generating less sulfur dioxide (Filonchyk & Hurynovich, 2020). Coal and crude oil usage also declined, reducing carbon oxide emissions. The reduction of transport activities in particular decreased the discharge amount of PM2.5 and PM10 (Bao & Zhang, 2020).

Renewable energies emerging in the face of COVID-19

The energy sector has always been fluctuating, but the safety measures surrounding it have created confidence, and comfortability in it. However, the arrival of COVID-19 and its sudden effects created chaos within this reliable sector. Sudden steep drops in oil prices and reduction in energy demand devastated industrial transport and conventional energy sources— while renewables remained stable against the sudden wreckage (Gollakota & Shu, 2022). Perhaps the confidence in conventional energy has been misplaced. Wind, solar, hydrothermal, hydrogen, and biomass-based energy systems remained in high gear. COVID-19 created the opportunity to highlight the efficacy of renewable energy and its steadiness in the face of crises.

The pandemic resulted in decreased economic pace and productive work, dropping the global demand for energy. The International Energy Agency estimated that there was a 3.8% decrease of energy demand in the first wave of COVID-19 (early-2020) and a further 6% decrease during the second wave (end-2020) (Renewable Energy Market Update, 2020). The economical aspects were astronomical, resulting in a financial crisis six to eight times greater than the 2008 Financial Crisis (Renewable Energy Market Update, 2020). Energy demand dropped globally, with the population accounting for 53% of energy consumption being in a lockdown in Europe, America, and Asia. Without an active service sector, the energy demand continued to further decrease. To combat this, many government systems implemented approaches to alleviate energy poverty by subsidizing electricity costs and ensuring all citizens have energy. In the wake of the pandemic's wreckage on the energy sector, an evaluation of energy-dependency by humans was conducted. The potentially lethal effects of a lack of energy, such as lack of hot water and heating, elevates our overreliance and importance of the energy sector. This urges for a reflection on the necessity of alternative energy sources and how it may not be a good idea to put all our eggs into non-renewable energy.

Due to the chaos in the energy sector caused by the reduction in energy demand, suspension of energy production, and distortion of energy prices, the vulnerability and limitations of the fossil fuel industry was realized. The volatile markets and prices, and high dependence on the labor force and a rigid production mode garnered interest in expanding the energy system outside of conventional energy sources. COVID-19 stimulated consideration into three main aspects of renewable energy (Zhang et al., 2021). First, the vulnerability of fossil fuels to extraneous factors makes renewable energy more appealing, inducing more investment interests as there are more stable production and maintenance costs. Second, renewable energy has more technical advantages compared to traditional energy sources, especially in the context of situations like COVID-19, where unforeseen emergencies require flexible production methods. Renewable energy provides a solution where decentralized production technologies allow for alternative energy resources and modes of production when the energy supply from conventional sources, which are centralized, is disrupted. Renewable energy can be dispatched before conventional electricity sources because of their lower operating costs. Renewable energy production is more resilient and allows for flexibility when facing lower electricity demand and energy generation by conventional sources can be reduced when there is an increase in renewable sources during the pandemic. Third, in exploration of renewable energy sources, a focus was placed on the internal reforms of the production and operational modes in the renewable energy sector. These reforms, while are on a much smaller scale, give a peek into the possible changes that can be implemented in the renewable energy sector. Farms began bio-energy production to diversify their production activities and make up for losses during the pandemic. Small companies in the renewable energy industry began merging into industry-purchasing groups to decrease costs. These reforms allow for a smooth transition from conventional energy sources to renewable energy sources on a wider scale, rather than a sudden shift that would disrupt production in both sources.

However, there are several negative consequences with the exploration into renewable energy during the pandemic. Global supply chains were disrupted and labour mobility was restricted across multiple sectors, this problem also largely affected the fossil fuel industry and posed the same problem and risk in renewable energy. For example, production and operations of solar photovoltaic modules and wind turbine components were disrupted. Consequently, exporter countries were unable to produce and export raw materials and semi-finished products for solar energy and wind energy for importer countries. Another problem arising from renewable energy is the lack of funding. While this is a persistent issue from before the pandemic, COVID-19 only worsened this. With relief funds being directed to the social needs and government revenue plummeting, the funds supporting renewable energy was scarce. This is further exacerbated by the shrinkage of energy demand during the pandemic, ultimately preventing the growth of the renewable energy industry.

During the COVID-19 pandemic, conventional energy sources realized the largest drop in consumption since 2009 whilst renewable energy and hydroelectricity consumption patterns showed an increasing pattern of +9.7% and 1.0%, respectively (Gollakota & Shu, 2022).

Impact of COVID-19 on the energy sector market

The lockdowns created a combination of both supply and demand shock. The supply shock stemmed from economic restrictions due to the closing down restaurants, in-store shopping, and factories. The demand shock stemmed from the skyrocketing need to stockpile for necessities such as toilet paper, masks, and emergency supplies. This supply and demand shock was evident in the increase in the share of energy consumption from 5% to 52% between mid-March and end-April (International Energy Agency, 2020).

The variation in energy consumption across global regions demonstrated that different regions were dependent on different primary energy sources. North, South, and Central America, and Europe were dependent on both natural gas and crude oil. Asia-Pacific was dependent on coal while the Middle East was dependent on natural gas (Gollakota & Shu, 2022). Using this variation, COVID-19 provided insight into the associations between oil prices and stock returns. The positive correlation between oil prices and inventory returns in the major Asian-Pacific net oil-importing countries was further strengthened by the pandemic (Prabheesh et al., 2020). The negative demand shock in the presence of a high economic uncertainty due from the drastic fall in oil prices during the pandemic resulted in economic instability. Energy companies faced negative performance in business with a higher fixed asset ratio and financial leverage bringing greater fixed and operating costs than any other sector (Gollakota & Shu, 2022). The decrease in energy demands and subsequently energy prices dropped the value of giant energy companies like BP. The unavoidable collapse in market value for the energy sector during times of crisis and the limited safety measures for this sector makes it a volatile investment, as COVID-19 reminded investors and shareholders. Unlike most sectors that have a safety net that can redirect sources of revenue, such as technical firms (Netflix, Zoom) or the service sector that can implement online models to overcome the pandemic, energy sectors (mining, heating) lack the capacity to do so. As such, the energy sector experienced the heaviest decline in stock value as they are unable to subsidize the loss of their primary source of revenue, suffering greater loss of earnings compared to other sectors.

The pandemic worsened the demand for resources across multiple sectors, disrupting the energy supply and energy market, especially the crude oil market. This disruption resulted in fluctuations in the energy market, which manifested in two main ways— volatility of energy prices and energy stock prices. To illustrate, Spain's electricity price in 2020 was 60% lower than expected and natural gas prices were 62% lower than expected (Abadie, 2021). Additionally, conflicts arose between main oil exporters and exacerbated oil sales prices, resulting in a sharper decline. In February of 2020, Brent crude oil prices declined 59% from the last crest value. Brent Crude represents the global benchmark for the trade oil market around Northwest Europe, encompassing 19 oil fields in the North Sea. This decline in oil prices was caused by the decline in oil demand, which continued supplying at a pre-pandemic rate. Thus, oil storage reached full capacity at petroleum storage facilities for the first time (Zhang et al., 2021). Accordingly, financial derivatives (ex. Oil futures) were so doff while storage capacity continued to run out, ultimately resulting in a large decline in oil prices. This fluctuation also produced the spillover effect, endangering the rest of the economy, especially shaking the economy of main energy exporters.

The established negative relation between oil prices and stock prices was threatened by COVID-19. Due to the sharp reduction in oil consumption because of lockdown measures, there was a decline in crude oil prices. Normally, the decline in oil prices reduces the cost of production, increasing stock prices due to the guaranteed higher future earnings and dividends (Zhang et al., 2021). However, during the COVID-19 pandemic, there was a trend of declining oil prices along with plunging stock markets, notably in oil-importing countries. This brings into question whether the relationship still holds and what factors would challenge this pattern.

Energy policies enacted during COVID-19

As the financial effects of the pandemic was felt on the population, governments were pressed to form public policies to lessen such burdens and support economic recovery. The goals of the new energy policies were divided into energy security policies and sustainable development policies (Zhang et al., 2021). Policymakers aimed to enact energy policies which influenced not only the energy industry, but also social, economic and environmental sectors as well. Non-core jobs that could not be done remotely were closed, resulting in unemployment. Accompanied by the increasing residential energy consumption due to the lockdown, economic burdens were increasing in low-income households and many communities faced problems of energy insecurity. Energy poverty increased, which encouraged unsafe heating behaviours such as using ovens and burning trash to overcome the harsh weather conditions. The provision of energy is a basic human right, thus energy policies were established to address energy poverty and insecurity in multiple nations. For example, the United States implemented the Low Income Home Energy Assistance Program.

Energy security of countries overly reliant on a single export such as crude oil and natural gas, was also threatened. The sudden and drastic revenue loss in the energy industry led to economic vulnerability nationally. However, the only increasing financial burden due to the increased demands of all the other sectors resulted in several countries unable to afford a large-scale relief policy, resulting in them having to turn to the international community for an assistance policy. Due to COVID-19, the excessive burden on a nation resulted in the changing dynamics between countries, where certain developing countries became indebted and financially dependent on other nations.

Economical impacts

Outbreaks of infectious diseases have always created a wobble in the economy, whether it be directly or indirectly. Case and point, the 2003 SARS outbreak reduced the consumption of different goods and services while increasing the demand for others, similar to COVID-19. Business operational costs were still increased despite the lack of profits, resulting in higher risk premiums for operations in regions with high infection risks. The anticipation for unknown highly infectious diseases lacking a vaccine significantly affected the economy and continues to do so (Lee & McKibbin, 2004). In the case of COVID-19, the economic impact was mainly caused by the decrease and shift in energy demand and its related sectors. There was a 4.5% decrease in overall primary consumption, the lowest since 2009. The largest contributor would be from oil energy sources, decreasing 9.7% (Gollakota & Shu, 2022). Large energy consumers North America, Europe, and Asia-Pacific scored the lowest in consumption trends: -8.0%, -7.8%, and -1.6% (Gollakota & Shu, 2022). Coal remained the second-largest fuel source in 2020, with 27.2% of the total primary consumption, while natural gas and renewable energy reached a record high at 24.7% and 5.7%, respectively (Gollakota & Shu, 2022).

Instability in the energy sector had an impact on the macroeconomy, especially as many sectors and industries were heavily dependent on it. The impact of this spillage depended on the roles of other countries. Fluctuations in the energy market for energy exporters led to macroeconomic pressure, with primary energy production and export reducing the national budget in the face of declined global demand during COVID-19. Furthermore, pessimism in future energy projections heavily impacted Russian and Saudi Arabia economies (Rostan & Rostan, 2020). Decreased demand and prices for oil had a different effect on macroeconomics for energy importers. For example, Turkey's GDP faced a decline of 1.16% due to decreased oil export and income gained from transportation and tertiary industry productions (Aydın & Ari, 2020).

References

Abadie, L. M. (2021). Energy Market Prices in Times of COVID-19: The Case of Electricity and Natural Gas in Spain. Energies, 14(6), 1632. https://doi.org/10.3390/en14061632

Ajami, N. K., & Kane, J. W. (2020, October 20). The hidden role of water infrastructure in driving a COVID-19 recovery. Brookings; The Brookings Institution. https://www.brookings.edu/blog/the-avenue/2020/10/20/the-hidden-role-of-water-infrastructure-in-driving-a-covid-19-recovery/

Aydın, L., & Ari, I. (2020). The impact of Covid-19 on Turkey's non-recoverable economic sectors compensating with falling crude oil prices: A computable general equilibrium analysis. Energy Exploration & Exploitation, 38(5), 014459872093400. https://doi.org/10.1177/0144598720934007

Bao, R., & Zhang, A. (2020). Does lockdown reduce air pollution? Evidence from 44 cities in northern China. Science of the Total Environment, 731, 139052. https://doi.org/10.1016/j.scitotenv.2020.139052

Butler, G., Pilotto, R. G., Hong, Y., & Mutambatsere, E. (2021). The Impact of COVID-19 on the Water and Sanitation Sector. International Finance Corporation.

Chakraborty, P., Jayachandran, S., Padalkar, P., Sitlhou, L., Chakraborty, S., Kar, R., Bhaumik, S., & Srivastava, M. (2020). Exposure to Nitrogen Dioxide (NO2) from Vehicular Emission Could Increase the COVID-19 Pandemic Fatality in India: A Perspective. Bulletin of Environmental Contamination and Toxicology, 105(2), 198–204. https://doi.org/10.1007/s00128-020-02937-3

Filonchyk, M., & Hurynovich, V. (2020). Spatial distribution and temporal variation of atmospheric pollution in the South Gobi Desert, China, during 2016–2019. Environmental Science and Pollution Research, 27(21), 26579–26593. https://doi.org/10.1007/s11356-020-09000-y

Gollakota, A. R. K., & Shu, C.-M. (2022). Covid-19 and energy sector: Unique opportunity for switching to clean energy. Gondwana Research. https://doi.org/10.1016/j.gr.2022.01.014

International Energy Agency. (2020). Global Energy Review 2020: The impacts of the Covid-19 crisis on global energy demand and CO2 emissions (p. 56). International Energy Agency.

Lee, J.-W., & McKibbin, W. J. (2004). Globalization and Disease: The Case of SARS. Asian Economic Papers, 3(1), 113–131. https://doi.org/10.1162/1535351041747932

Nižetić, S. (2020). Impact of coronavirus (COVID-19) pandemic on air transport mobility, energy, and environment: A case study. International Journal of Energy Research, 44(13). https://doi.org/10.1002/er.5706

Prabheesh, K. P., Padhan, R., & Garg, B. (2020). COVID-19 and the oil price – stock market nexus: Evidence from net oil-importing countries. Energy RESEARCH LETTERS, 1(2). https://doi.org/10.46557/001c.13745
Renewable energy market update. (2020). International Energy Agency.

Rostan, P., & Rostan, A. (2020). Where is Saudi Arabia's economy heading? International Journal of Emerging Markets, 16(8). https://doi.org/10.1108/ijoem-08-2018-0447

Zhang, L., Li, H., Lee, W.-J., & Liao, H. (2021). COVID-19 and energy: Influence mechanisms and research methodologies. Sustainable Production and Consumption, 27, 2134–2152. https://doi.org/10.1016/j.spc.2021.05.010

Chapter 8
How Covid-19 has reshaped the primary care physician-patient relationship

By Dollyann Santhosh

Introduction

Let us begin by playing out a scene that many are familiar with: you have decided to book an appointment with your family doctor. You are lucky enough to have this specific physician be your designated family doctor - a luxury that many do not have even in the era of modern medicine as we know it. You arrive at the clinic, and are promptly seated in an examination room to wait for your doctor. Once they arrive, you exchange familiar smiles and take a few minutes to catch up on how life has been. The environment is relaxed and comfortable - you know you are in the presence of someone who you have already established a comfortable physician-patient relationship with. They know a great deal about you and your health, and once you bring up your main concern, the physician's questions are rather simple and direct. Together, you are able to discuss your chief complaints and arrive at a mutually agreed upon course of action to address your concerns.

The Foundations of the Patient-Physician Relationship

Roter (2000) describes how in a much similar way to the science of medicine has been advancing, so have the intricacies and nuances of the patient-physician relationship. Medicine has shifted away from its paternalistic forefathers and now fosters a collaborative model where patients (and their physicians!) are encouraged to advocate for their interests. It has been said that there is an art to medicine. Meaning, despite established regimens, protocols and therapeutic margins, the physician's judgment is integral in coming up with a plan that is best suited to the needs of the patient. The prudent physician not only considers the best course of action physiologically, but also incorporates key aspects of the patient's values. Survival or optimizing health may not be a priority for all, given their circumstance and their individual health. For instance, comfort care could be a priority for patients with end-stage cancer however recovery and return to baseline functionality is a more likely priority for those with acute conditions.

But, how exactly does a physician navigate the intricacies of patient priorities? This is where the importance of longitudinal patient-physician relationships are highlighted. Roter elaborates that the patient-physician relationship can be described in 5 main ways: as being "medically functional, informative, facilitative, responsive, and participatory" (2000). Of course, the degree to which each of these characteristics can be applied to a patient visit varies greatly, but generally speaking are descriptive of interactions of this nature. In being medically functional, the patient visit addresses the chief complaint(s) that brought the individual in to see the physician. It is possible but not certain that the presenting illness is resolved, or even diagnosed, within one visit; however it is the attempts that the physician makes to arrive at the most appropriate diagnosis and intervention, in partnership with the patient that describes the interaction as being medically functional. An informative patient visit can be functionally described as one where a patient is able to leave the physician's office with a clear and succinct understanding of what their condition could be, the course of action to manage their condition, and a general understanding of what is/could be going on with their health. A key marker of an informative patient visit is a mutual understanding between the patient and the physician about the current state of the patient's health.

According to Roter, the visit must also be facilitative such that the patient-physician interaction is able to facilitate the patient's ability to tell the story of [their] illness" (2000). The ability to facilitate the telling of their story lays on the foundation that is the relationship between the patient and their physician. Establishing trust, good rapport, and creating a welcoming atmosphere that allows the patient to feel vulnerable enough to share the history of their presenting illness is a direct example of the importance of the patient-physician relationship. In establishing a solid foundation with the patient, it assists the physician in getting a full understanding of the patient's illness experience; in other words, how the presenting illness is affecting them in the context of their life and their day-to-day functioning. We must then also consider how the patient-physician relationship is understood as being "responsive" (Roter, 2000). It is of the utmost importance to consider that the physician tends to the patient - not only the patient's concerns. Recognizing that it takes a patient a considerable amount of vulnerability to openly share the history of their presenting illness is the mark of a conscientious physician. Thereby, in establishing a strong patient-physician relationship, the medical doctor is able to create an environment where the patient feels validated, supported, seen and heard.

Lastly, but certainly not the least, the physician-patient relationship is described as being participatory by Roter (2000). As previously alluded to, medicine has taken large strides away from its previous paternalistic models. The contemporary model physician includes and encourages the patient to be a part of the decision-making process. It can be argued that this is a key principle of the patient-provider interaction especially when it comes to treatment selection and their subsequent outcomes. In prescribing a treatment regimen that is incompatible with the patient's lifestyle or fails to consider complexities of their life, may lead to exacerbation of the existing illness or may even expose the patient to further complications. For example, in HIV+ patients, treatment adherence is of the utmost importance in order to prevent the resurfacing of disease symptoms and HIV strain mutations leading to drug resistance (HIV Info, 2021, Adherence section). Therefore, selection of treatment options can have mild to life-threatening implications thus emphasizing the importance of involving patients and their interests in discussions of illness management.

However, the artful incorporation of all these characteristics can be argued as being achieved through longitudinal relationships between patients and their physicians. The creation of a safe space, good professional rapport, and understanding is something that comes from repeated visits and multilayered conversations. Not only are established longitudinal relationships beneficial from a provider point of view such that physicians are able to understand the social context of their patients and provide better medical care, they are also beneficial from a patient perspective - it understandably easier to share intimate details and the complex impact of illness experiences with someone whom you know and trust.

Another key aspect of the patient-physician interaction is the non-verbal communication that occurs during the visit. In fact, many medical schools make incorporating non-verbal communication in patient interactions a key component of medical education (Vogel et. al., 2018). Non-verbal cues play an important role in fostering a comfortable space for patients to be comfortable and vulnerable thus shaping the interaction to be facilitative and responsive. There are a number of behavioral and paraverbal cues that are employed by physicians and encouraged by medical schools to achieve this effect. Some examples include, the use of open body language (displayed by facing the patient directly, leaning forward), use of eye contact, meaningful nodding to affirm the patient and confirm that the physician is engaged in the discourse. Paraverbal cues however include nuances of the voice - these can include aspects such as the tone, pitch, and pace of speech as the patient and physician engage in discussion.

Let us go back to our scenario to demonstrate the intricacies of these interactions. You are seated in the examination room and you notice that you are slightly worried about how this doctor's visit will go. After all, there is always a possibility that your concerns are more serious than you initially thought. After a few minutes, the physician enters the room with a slight knock and a warm smile. They greet you with a soft, familiar smile and a gentle voice that accompanies it. Seeing your physician's familiar face and their gentle demeanor has already helped calm you down a considerable amount. The conversation begins with ease - you are asked about how life is going, your job, your family, etc. And as your doctor listens, they sit facing you and enthusiastically nod along to your responses. You feel as though their concern and interest in your general well-being is genuine and consequently, you feel much more ready to discuss the reason for your visit. The physician senses your readiness, and asks you "What brings you in today?", allowing you to begin the story of how your chief complaint began. You are not rushed, and the physician's sole attention to you and your story encourages you to divulge more details of not only the complaint, but also how it has been impacting your life and daily functioning.

As demonstrated, it is easy to imagine that the shaping of a longitudinal physician-patient in large is influenced by recurrent and consistent follow-ups as well as the influences of non-verbal communication that impacts how a patient feels in the presence of their physician.

With the advent of the COVID-19 pandemic, it is undeniable that there have been substantial changes to the way the world functions, with a special emphasis on the way modern healthcare functions. Acute care centers like emergency departments have obviously felt the burden of such drastic changes; however, there have been a number of changes to the primary care setting that has impacted the traditional formation and maintenance of patient-physician relationships.

The effects of the pandemic

In order to explore the various ways in which the COVID-19 pandemic has affected the relationship between doctors and patients, a bottom-up approach may be most effective.

Let us add a few key changes to the scenario painted for us. Prior to booking your appointment with your primary care physician, you are asked a number of questions by the receptionist - a series of questions screening you for apparent COVID-19 symptoms.

You arrive at the clinic and are greeted by a number of masked individuals. You are asked the same series of questions once again, your temperature is measured, and you are given a mask to wear yourself. Once you are seated in the examination room, you sense a very drastic change in the atmosphere of your once familiar family medicine clinic. There is a sense of weariness and distance; you find it hard to connect with the individuals around you and this is partly exacerbated by the fact that it is much harder to read their facial expressions with masks on. You wait a few moments, and are once again greeted by your familiar family physician; however, the setting no longer feels familiar. Your physician arrives in attire you are unfamiliar with - a gown, face mask, face shield, and gloves. They greet you as they always have, but there is considerable distance maintained between you and your physician. Though the greetings and the words seem routine, they do not feel that way. You realize you miss the visual cues that once put you at ease in the presence of your physician - the warm smiles, a gentle softening of their face as you describe your chief complaint, it is even hard at times to hear the exact words of your doctor as their speech sounds muffled through their personal protective equipment. You sense a new environment of urgency - from the physician perspective, limiting contact and contact time is rather important. Though you are present in the clinic, in order to maintain safety for both yourself and your doctor, you sense they are trying to spend as little time in the examination room as possible. Your chief complaint has been discussed, and for the most part your needs are met however you sense a lack of connection with your physician that was once very comforting.

As demonstrated above, even from the most basic point of view, the pandemic has had small yet impactful effects on the communication between physicians and their patients - it is not unreasonable to assume that the changes in interaction have thus also impacted the rapport between physicians and their patients. Even patients that have had relationships with their physicians on the order of decades may have felt a sudden shift in those relationships as the result of the COVID-19 pandemic. Ghosh et. al. describe how distancing between patients and providers contribute to physical safety as well as a sense of safety for both patients and physicians however on the other hand may reduce feelings of connection and privacy (due to the need to speak loudly to overcome the distance and muffling from masks) (2021). As previously described, the social and emotional aspects of the medical consult are of the utmost importance in a primary care setting as they not only function to put the patient at ease, but also aid the physician in creating a welcoming atmosphere that allows the patient to tell them the history of presenting illness in an effective and comprehensive manner. In the new context of the COVID-19 pandemic, primary care physicians are forced to overcome these challenges and continue to build or maintain rapport with their patients while balancing the need for safety and distance.

The rise of telemedicine

One may argue that one of the biggest gifts of the 21st century has been the development of outstanding technology. Not only have these technologies been radically improved themselves, but have also been made easily accessible for the general public. It is this combination of powerful technology and accessibility that has transformed the current world (and healthcare system) as we know it today.

It is precisely the technology as we know that helped the world navigate the complexities of the COVID-19 pandemic. Many cite access to technology as being a key factor in maintaining connections with the outside world especially when quarantining during the first phase of the pandemic. It is also the same technology that allowed primary care physicians to overcome some of the challenges of the pandemic, especially in the beginning stages. Non-emergent cases had the potential to be addressed as phone consults rather than in person visits, thus primary care providers jumped at the opportunity. Telemedicine proved to be much more convenient, especially from the provider point of view however it was not without caveats of its own. However telemedicine came with challenges of its own - according to one study, some physicians were concerned about patients who did not have access to technology and thus were not able to access care (Gomez, et. al. 2021). For some, it was not the access to technology but rather the lack of knowledge or expertise to use said technology that posed a challenge (elderly populations are one such example). So, although telemedicine offered a temporary solution to distancing, especially in the first phases of the pandemic, it arguably offered a different approach to primary care that has disadvantages of its own.

Downsides of Virtual Medical Care

Let us consider another example. An elderly patient that lives alone schedules regular monthly appointments with their family doctor. The patient does not necessarily always have pressing concerns, but seems to rather enjoy their visits with their physician as it provides an opportunity for interaction and connection. Loneliness is a pressing issue especially among elderly patients (Donaldson & Watson, 1996). Though the physician may not be directly caring for this patient's physical health in any apparent way, it can be argued that they are a big contributor to this patient's mental wellbeing and therefore are contributing to promoting the overall health of this patient.

In this context, telemedicine may not be able to remedy all. Loneliness has serious implications in overall health, especially for elderly patients (Dahlberg, 2021). Once again, though telemedicine may be able to transiently address pressing concerns for patients, they lack many factors of the patient-physician interaction that contributes to feelings of good rapport and connection. For elderly patients (such as the individual highlighted in the example) telemedicine may fail to achieve the key purpose of doctor's visits.

Another pressing concern of telemedicine for physicians is the potential for misdiagnosis, or even worse, the potential for missing presentations of serious conditions or complications. A key component of the patient consultation is the physical examination. To the medically trained eyes, seemingly unremarkable findings could indicate much more serious complications or clinically relevant pathophysiology. A major barrier of telemedicine is the inability to perform a physical exam on the patient (Gajarawala & Pelowski, 2021). A skilled physician chooses to perform a physical examination based on the history provided by the patient, but also physical characteristics that they notice during the patient encounter. During a phone consultation however, the physician is forced to depend solely on descriptions from the patient. Not only does this strain the limits of clinical judgment, it also places a burden on the patient to report on symptoms or findings that may not necessarily deem important or relevant. There is a potential then to miss key presentations of illness that may guide the diagnosis process in a certain direction. It is also important to recognize that sometimes it is quite likely that one may report feeling healthy despite having serious pathophysiologies - in essence, it is possible to feel fine while still being very sick. The in-person patient-physician interaction reduces the chances of such instances being missed, once again, because the physical presence of the physician allows them to evaluate and examine the patient themself.

Changes to Clinical Thinking

It is undeniable that the global community was forced to adapt to the new world that was the result of the COVID-19 pandemic, and changes in clinical thinking by physicians was part of this adaptation. Respiratory symptoms had to be given special thought - the attentive physician was expected to know when and how to differentiate between the effects of the COVID-19 virus as opposed to other respiratory illnesses, and also to recognize when complications due to the COVID-19 virus were posing a serious threat. Physicians were put in an interesting position where there was a very limited amount of information available on the disease itself, but also how it was expected to manifest in patients, and long term implications. One may describe the position of physicians as 'blind mice in a maze'.

In Conclusion

Considering the barriers of telemedicine combined with changes to clinical thinking and reduced interaction with patients, the COVID-19 pandemic has drastically changed the face of primary care medicine from a physician perspective. Key aspects of the physician-patient interaction and relationship were dramatically altered or altogether eliminated due to the pandemic. Interactive foundations of the patient-physician relationship such as nonverbal communication and rapport building were dampened due to the limitations of social distancing and personal protective equipment. And, from a clinical perspective, the way physicians traditionally practiced medicine also changed. Important indicators such as the physical presentation and demeanor of a patient became absent in the context of telemedicine, forcing physicians to critically consider the history of presenting illness provided to them by their patient. Not only were these intricacies apparent in the immediate sense, but they have had long-standing implications for the way primary care physicians view their practice and perhaps even train the future generation of primary care physicians.

References

Vogel, D., Meyer, M. & Harendza, S. Verbal and non-verbal communication skills including empathy during history taking of undergraduate medical students. BMC Med Educ 18, 157 (2018). https://doi.org/10.1186/s12909-018-1260-9

Buller, M. K., & Buller, D. B. (1987). Physicians' Communication Style and Patient Satisfaction. Journal of Health and Social Behavior, 28(4), 375–388. https://doi.org/10.2307/2136791

Makoul, G. PhD. (2001). Essential Elements of Communication in Medical Encounters: The Kalamazoo Consensus Statement. Academic Medicine, 76(4), 390-393 '

Olaisen, H.R., Schluchter, M. D., Flocke, S. A., Smyth, K. A., Koroukian, S. M., Stange, K. C., (2020). Assessing the Longitudinal Impact of Physician-Patient Relationship on Functional Health. The Annals of Family Medicine, 18(5), 422-429; DOI: https://doi.org/10.1370/afm.2554

U.S. Department of Health and Human Services. (2021, August). HIV treatment adherence. National Institutes of Health. Retrieved December 4, 2022, from https://hivinfo.nih.gov/understanding-hiv/fact-sheets/hiv-treatment-adherence#:~:text=Why%20is%20medication%20adherence%20important,resistance%20and%20HIV%20treatment%20failure

Davis B, Bankhead-Kendall BK, Dumas RP. (2022). A review of COVID-19's impact on modern medical systems from a health organization management perspective. Health Technol (Berl), 12(4), 815-824. doi: 10.1007/s12553-022-00660-z. Epub 2022 Mar 25. PMID: 35371904; PMCID: PMC8956330

Roter, D. (2000). The enduring and evolving nature of the patient-physician relationship. Patient Education and Counseling, 39(1), 5-15

Drouvelis, M. & Grosskopf, B. (2021). The impact of smiling cues on social cooperation. Southern Economic Journal, 87(4), 1390-1404; https://doi.org/10.1002/soej.12485

Xu B. (2022). The impact of COVID-19 on the doctor-patient relationship in China. Front Public Health. 10: 907009; doi: 10.3389/fpubh.2022.907009

Wang Y, Wu Q, Wang Y, Wang P. (2022). The Effects of Physicians' Communication and Empathy Ability on Physician-Patient Relationship from Physicians' and Patients' Perspectives. J Clin Psychol Med Settings, 29(4):849-860. doi: 10.1007/s10880-022-09844-1. Epub 2022 Jan 28. PMID: 35089529; PMCID: PMC8795960

Chipidza FE, Wallwork RS, Stern TA. (2015). Impact of the Doctor-Patient Relationship. Prim Care Companion CNS Disord, 17(5):10.4088/PCC.15f01840. doi: 10.4088/PCC.15f01840. PMID: 26835164; PMCID: PMC4732308.

Anderson JG, Rainey MR, Eysenbach G. (2003). The impact of CyberHealthcare on the physician-patient relationship. J Med Syst, 27(1), 67-84. doi: 10.1023/a:1021061229743. PMID: 12617199. Emanuel EJ, Emanuel LL. (1992). Four Models of the Physician-Patient Relationship. JAMA, 267(16), 2221–2226. doi:10.1001/jama.1992.03480160079038

Ball MJ, Lillis J.(2001). E-health: transforming the physician/patient relationship. Int J Med Inform, 61(1), 1-10; doi: 10.1016/s1386-5056(00)00130-1. PMID: 11248599

Johanson, D. L., Ahn, H. S., Sutherland, C. J., Brown, B., Macdonald, B., Lim, J. Y., Ahn, B. K., Broadbent, E. (2020). Smiling and use of first-name by a healthcare receptionist robot: Effects on user perceptions, attitudes, and behaviours. Paladyn, Journal of Behavioral Robotics, 11(1), 40-51; DOI: 10.1515/pjbr-2020-0008

Macdonald, D. M., Berv, J. (2022). Losing Contact — Covid-19, Telemedicine, and the Patient–Provider Relationship. New England Journal of Medicine, 387, 775-777; DOI: 10.1056/NEJMp2206471

McCrackin, S. D., Capozzi, F., Mayrand, F., Ristic, J. (2022). Face Masks Impair Basic Emotion Recognition. Social Psychology; Doi:https://doi.org/10.1027/1864-9335/a000470

Ghosh, A., Sharma, K., Choudhury, S. (2021). COVID-19 and physician–patient relationship: potential effects of 'masking', 'distancing' and 'others'. Family Practice, 38(2), 192-193; https://doi.org/10.1093/fampra/cmaa092

Donaldson J. M., Watson, R. (1996). Loneliness in elderly people: an important area for nursing research. J Adv Nurs, 24(5):952-9; doi: 10.1111/j.1365-2648.1996.tb02931.x. PMID: 8933255.

Dahlberg, L. (2021). Loneliness during the COVID-19 pandemic. Aging Mental Health, 25(7): 1161-1164; doi: 10.1080/13607863.2021.1875195. Epub 2021 Jan 25. PMID: 33491474.

Gajarawala S.N., Pelkowski J. N. (2021). Telehealth Benefits and Barriers. J Nurse Pract, 17(2):218-221; doi: 10.1016/j.nurpra.2020.09.013. Epub 2020 Oct 21. PMID: 33106751; PMCID: PMC7577680

Kahn J. M. (2015). Virtual visits--confronting the challenges of telemedicine. New England Journal of Medicine, 372(18):1684-1685; doi: 10.1056/NEJMp1500533. PMID: 25923547

Wanat M, Hoste M, Gobat N, Anastasaki M, Böhmer F, Chlabicz S, Colliers A, Farrell K, Karkana MN, Kinsman J, Lionis C, Marcinowicz L, Reinhardt K, Skoglund I, Sundvall PD, Vellinga A, Verheij TJ, Goossens H, Butler CC, van der Velden A, Anthierens S & Tonkin-Crine S. (2021). Transformation of primary care during the COVID-19 pandemic: experiences of healthcare professionals in eight European countries. British Journal of General Practice, 71(709):e634-e642; doi: 10.3399/BJGP.2020.1112. PMID: 33979303; PMCID: PMC8274627.

Chapter 9
The Effects of COVID-19 on Asian Hate Crime

By Jason Zhou

Throughout history, pandemic-related health crises have commonly been associated with stigmatization of individuals of Asian descent. The Coronavirus Disease 2019 (COVID-19) is believed to have emerged in Wuhan, China. As the virus began rapidly spreading around the world, sinophobia - the fear of Chinese people - became widespread. Despite the World Health Organization (WHO) having a specific guidance about not naming disease after specific places, many media outlets began using headlines such as "Yellow peril", "Chinese virus panda-monium", and "China kids stay home" (Sharma, 2021). This behaviour of xenophobia was further motivated with Donald Trump, the former President of the United States, referring to COVID-19 as the "Chinese virus", "Wuhan virus", and "Kung flu" (Sharma, 2021). This led to a surge in racially motivated hate crimes involving physical violence and harassment towards individuals of Asian descent.

What is a Hate Crime?

There is not a universal classification and definition of a hate crime, instead each country has their own definition of a hate crime, which makes what constitutes a hate crime highly variable. In the United States, a hate crime is defined as "any unlawful action designed to frighten, harm, injure, intimidate or harass an individual, in whole or in part, because of a bias motivation against the actual or perceived race, religion, ethnic background or sexual orientation of the victim" and "an act which appears to be motivated or perceived to be motivated by the victim based on race, religion or ethic background" (Government of Canada, 2022). In Canada, some police forces have their own definition of a hate crime, while others use definitions provided from bias crime guidelines. The Metropolitan Toronto Police Force defines a hate crime as "a criminal offence committed against a person or property that is based solely upon the victim's race, religion, nationality, ethnic origin, sexual orientation, gender or disability" (Government of Canada, 2022). The Ottawa Police Service defines a hate crime as "a criminal offence committed against a person or property which is motivated by the suspect/offender's hate/bias against a racial, religious, ethnic, sexual orientation or disability group" (Government of Canada, 2022). The Ministry of the Solicitor General / Correctional Service of Canada states the definition as "crime was motivated because of has/bias toward the victim's racial religious, ethnic or sexual orientation" (Government of Canada, 2022). The Policing Standards Manual of the Province of Ontario states that a hate crime is "a criminal offence committed against a person or property which is motivated by the suspect/offender's hate/bias against a racial, religious, ethnic, sexual orientation or disability group" (Government of Canada, 2022). The Ontario Provincial Police provides the following definition of a hate crime, "a criminal act against a person(s) or property that is based solely, or in part, upon the victim's race, religion, ethnicity, sexual orientation or disability" (Government of Canada, 2022). With so many varying definitions of a hate crime, it creates an argument for what exactly is a hate crime and it is in part why obvious racially motivated acts of violences are not ruled as hate crimes.

Xenophobia Seen in Past Pandemics

Looking at pandemics throughout history, there is often a misguided belief that 'outsiders' are more susceptible to contracting disease and infecting others as they are perceived to be poorer, less hygienic, and consume strange foods (Sharma, 2021). An example of such xenophobia is seen in 1916 with the Polio outbreak. The initial cases of polio were in an Italian neighbourhood in South Brooklyn called "Pig Town" as the neighborhood was surrounded by piles of garbage and free-roaming pigs. As the number of polio cases drastically rose, resulting in the death or paralyzation of many infants, a wave of anti-Italian prejudice began. Heavily armed policemen patrolled roads and rail stations to prevent Italians from leaving the city and health officers went door to door to enforce isolation measures and hospitalization. Many wealthy estate owners - former American President Theodore Roosevelt being one of them - blamed poor Italian residents for the polio epidemic and made police officers seize children and issue fines for uncollected trash (Sharma, 2021).

Similar to COVID-19, smallpox was believed to have originated from China. So in 1871, when British Columbia joined the Canadian Confederation and the Canadian government began a system to recruit and hire thousands of Chinese laborers to build the Canadian Pacific Railway, many of these Chinese people faced discrimination by the white communities in the area (Sharma, 2021). This discrimination was further motivated as Canada passed the Chinese Immigration Act in 1885 which placed a "head tax" on the Chinese laborers (Sharma, 2021). Quarantine officers were also stationed at all ports to inspect any individual of Chinese origin and examine any Chinese person suspected to be ill.

A more recent example is seen with Ebola in 2014. BBC reported many instances of racism following the initial outbreak of Ebola in West Africa. For instance, a school in New Jersey sent two Rwandan students back to their home country for no apparent reason (Sharma, 2021). Another college in Texas stopped accepting applications from Nigeria, stating it was due to the country having confirmed cases of Ebola. However, at that time, there were no longer active cases of Ebola in Nigeria. Additionally, the outbreak of Ebola was during a time when social media began becoming prevalent in everyone's daily life. This allowed for people to easily spread racist and xenophobic comments, similar to how media has encouraged the anti-Asian behaviour.

Hate Crimes During COVID-19 in Canada

The Chinese Canadian National Council Toronto Chapter (CNCTO) and a grassroots organization called Project 1907, conducted a survey and found that there were 943 reports of racist incidents across Canada in 2021, which is a 47 per cent increase compared to 2020 (Balintec, 2022). It was found that women submitted and continue to submit the majority of complaints. However, in addition, the number of complaints submitted by children and adolescents increased by 286 per cent over the past year (Balintec, 2022). Violent attacks also continue to occur, with a 42 per cent increase in the number of Asians being coughed at or spat on (Balintec, 2022). According to the report by CNCTO and Project 1907, more than 80 per cent of the individuals that reported an incident are simply looking for either more public education, collective action or policy reform instead of their aggressors, 75 percent of whom were white men, facing consequences or apologizing for their actions (Balintec, 2022). The report also offered some solutions to aid in the fight against xenophobia. Some of these solutions include more long term funding for Asian community organizations, the creation of trauma informed, culturally, and linguistically accessible anti-racism programs, more representation of Asian women in decision-making processes, and the passing of Ontario's Bill 86 which states specific actions to combat hate crimes (Balintec, 2022).

Instances of Hate Crimes During COVID-19 in the United States
Since the beginning of the COVID-19 pandemic, there has been an increase in violent hate crimes against people of Asian descent, the most infamous one being the mass shooting in Atlanta, Georgia. On March 16, 2021, 21 year old Robert Aaron Long began the shooting at Young's Asian Massage in a northwest suburb of Atlanta which resulted in four fatalities. Long then continued the shooting at a second spa called Gold Spa where the Atlanta police later found three women with gunshot wounds. While the officers were at Gold Spa, they received a report of shots being fired at another spa, Aromatherapy Spa, across the street, where another fatality occurred. The eight victims were Delaina Ashley Yuan, 33; Paul Andre Michels, 54; Xiaojie Tan, 49; Daoyou Feng, 44; Soon Chung Park, 74; Hyun Jung Grant, 51; Suncha Kim, 69; and Yong Ae Yue, 63 (Chavez & Chen, 2022). Of the eight total victims, six of them were Asian American women. Many members of the general public

considered this a violent and targeted hate crime against Asian American women. This sparked fear and concern among the Asian American community, especially during a time where racism and discrimination were spiking due to the COVID-19 pandemic. The police had caught Long on his way to Florida with plans to carry out a similar violence. During an interview about the shooting, the Cherokee County sheriff's deputy, Captain Jay Baker, spoke about the shooter and said "he was pretty much fed up and had been kind of at the end of his rope, yesterday was a really bad day for him, and this is what he did" (Graham, 2021). This statement was spread widely across social media, with many people criticizing Captain Baker and characterizing him as callous. Social media users found Facebook posts from March 30 and April 2, 2020 by Captain Baker in which he promoted the sale of anti-Asian shirts and referred to COVID-19 as "an imported virus from Chy-na" (Graham, 2021). Captain Baker's casual and open acts of racism resulted in individuals requesting he be removed from his job; however, the Cherokee County Sheriff, Frank Reynolds, defended Captain Baker, saying he did not intend to disrespect the victims or express empathy or sympathy for the suspect (Graham, 2021). Long was charged with eight counts of murder and one count of aggravated assault, claiming that he had a "sexual addiction" and had carried out the shootings at the spas to eliminate his "temptation" (Graham, 2021). These charges sparked outrage among the Asian Americans as they felt that the state and federal courts were ignoring a deliberate act of anti-Asian racism.

Even before the Atlanta spa shooting occurred, many Asian Americans were facing harassment and after the shooting, these attacks have only increased. On January 19, 2021, a 68 year old Vietnamese woman, Hoa Nguyen, was punched in the face by a stranger on her way to a supermarket in Brooklyn. The stranger punched her two more times before walking away. The suspect was 51 year old Mercel Jackson who was charged with assault, harassment, and hate crime charges. Jackson told the police he "doesn't like how Chinese people look", "Chinese people look like measles," and "doesn't like Chinese people looking at him" (Chavez

& Chen, 2022). This incident had left Nguyen afraid to walk on the streets. In November of 2021, a 61 year old Asian woman, GuiYing Ma, was sweeping the sidewalk of an empty property in Jackson Heights when a stranger allegedly repeatedly stuck her in the head with a large rock (Vera & Reilly, 2022). The New York Police Department later arrested a 33 year old man named Elisaul Perez. He was charged with assault with intent to disfigure and dismember, assault with intent to seriously injure someone with a weapon, and criminal possession of a weapon. The attack left Ma with permanent damage to the right side of her brain. She woke up from her coma about 10 weeks after the attack but passed away shortly after due to complications from the head injury. These are only two examples of aggressive harassment and assault that individuals of Asian descent have been facing since the beginning of the COVID-19 pandemic. In New York alone, there were 131 incidents in 2021 confirmed to be anti-Asian crimes by the NYPD, which was a significant increase compared to the 27 incidents reported in 2020 and one in 2019 (Chavez & Chen, 2022). However, there are many cases of racism that are not reported. Between March 19, 2020 and September 30, 2021, 10, 370 hate incidents have been reported to Stop Asian American and Pacific Islander Hate (Stop AAPI Hate), an organization that allows individuals to self-report incidents of anti-Asian racism and discrimination.

Why Hate Crime Charges Are Rare

In February 2021, near Manhattan's Chinatown neighbourhood, a Chinese man was walking home when a stranger suddenly ran up behind him and stabbed his back (Hong & Bromwich, 2021). This stranger was 23 year old Salman Muflehi from Yemen who had not spoken a word to the victim before the attack (Hong & Bromwich, 2021). The prosecutors stated they lacked enough evidence to prove the attack was racially motivated, hence the attacker was charged with attempted murder but not as a hate crime. This ruling outraged many Asian Americans in New York, with many feeling as though racist assaults are being overlooked by the authorities. With many incidents not leading to arrests or not being charged as hate crimes, there is not reliable data to show the extent that members of the

Asian community are being targeted. It is particularly difficult to prove that an attack against Asians is racially motivated because there is no recognizable pattern with anti-Asian crimes (Hong & Bromwich, 2021). Historically, most crimes against Asians were small-business owners being robbed. This complicates the question of whether the motive was racism or money. Stewart Loo, a deputy inspector at the New York Police Department's Asian Hate Crimes Task Force, stated that Asian-Americans are often reluctant to report a crime because of language barriers, concerns over having their immigration papers questioned, fear of retaliation from perpetrators or simply do not want to cause trouble (Hong & Bromwich, 2021). Instead, many members of the Asian community rather have perpetrators be educated on anti-racism as putting someone in jail does not make them stop hating people of a certain race or ethnicity.

Stop Asian American and Pacific Islander (AAPI) Hate

In response to the escalation of xenophobia and bigotry resulting from the COVID-19 pandemic, three organizations, AAPI Equity Alliance (formerly A3PCON), Chinese for Affirmative Action (CAA), and the Asian Amercian Studies Department of San Francisco State University launched the Stop AAPI Hate coalition on March 19, 2020. The mission of this organization is "to advance equity, justice, and power by dismantling systemic racism and building a multiracial movement to end anti-Asian American and Pacific Islander (AAPI) hate" (Stop AAPI Hate, 2021). The Stop AAPI Hate website allows users to report incidents of hate crimes which the organization uses to actively track anti-Asian and Pacific Islander hate incidents to better understand what is happening, where, and to whom. The information that is collected is analyzed and used to advocate for resources and effective solutions. The organization also advocates for the passage of local, state, and national policies that strength human and civil rights protections, dismantle systemic racism that harm AAPI communities, and address the root causes of discrimination and bigotry. They also partner with other organizations to change how issues of racism are understood, build a plan to dismantle systemic racism and educate the general public on how anti-AAPI hate is a long-standing issue that requires people to stand in solidarity for equity for all. Some of the key initiatives of Stop AAPI Hate are to strength civil rights laws and enforcements so that all people are protected from discrimination and bias at places of business, public places, online and in schools; to provide people who have experienced hate with support; and to build a movement for education on Asian American and Pacific Islander and Black, Indigenous and People of Colour (BIPOC) issues and histories, and advancing ethnic studies.

Asian Americans Advancing Justice (AAJC)

Asian Americans Advancing Justice (AAJC) is an organization founded in 1991 that is dedicated to advancing civil and human rights for Asian Americans and to building a fair and equitable society for everyone (Asian Americans Advancing Justice, n.d.). AAJC is an affiliation of five organizations: Asian Americans Advancing Justice (Washington, DC), Asian Americans Advancing Justice - Asian Law Caucus, Asian Americans Advancing Justice - Atlanta, Asian Americans Advancing Justice - Chicago, and Asian Americans Advancing Justice - Southern California (Asian Americans Advancing Justice, n.d.). AAJC (Washington, DC) is the national location. AAJC - Asian Law Caucus is located in San Francisco and it is the United States's oldest legal organization defending the civil rights of members of the AAPI community, particularly those of low-income, immigrant and underserved communities. AAJC - Atlanta is the first non-profit law center dedicated to Asian immigrants and refugees in the southeast of the United States. AAJC - Atlanta also has the goal to educate, engage, and empower under-represented individuals of the AAPI community to have greater civil participation. AAJC - Chicago is the leading pan-Asian organization in the midwest of the United States and the organization is dedicated to empowering the AAPI community through advocacy, research, education, and coalition-building. AAJC - Southern California is the United States's largest legal organization that serves people in the AAPI community through direct legal services, impact litigation, policy advocacy, and leadership development. With the sharp increase in physical and mental health harms against Asian Americans, AAJC has been working to raise awareness about the increased racism and discrimination against people of Asian descent being wrongly accused as the cause of the COVID-19 pandemic.

Ways to Support the Fight Against Anti-Asian Violence

In this fight against the AAPI communities, there are many ways to help. One way of doing so is to donate to Stop AAPI Hate on their website. Stop AAPI Hate uses these donations to help support these initiatives and track and respond to instances of racism and xenophobia to the AAPI community. Another method to support the cause is to speak out if you witness a hate crime or incident, instead of being a bystander. If the situation becomes violent or a person's safety is in danger, you should report the incident to the police immediately. Another way to support the movement is by educating yourself on how to stop anti-Asian and xenophobic harrassment when you see it. One method to educate yourself is by attending training, specifically the bystander intervention training AAJC hosts in collaboration with Hollaback! (Ramachandran, 2021). You can also support the AAPI community by checking in on any members of the AAPI community in your life. In such a time where many people of Asian descent are afraid to leave their home, a gesture, such as offering to help them run an errand or asking about their well-being, helps them feel reassured that they are part of a larger community (Ramachandran, 2021). Equitable care is crucial towards societal development, particularly amid global pandemics and social crises.

References

Asian Americans Advancing Justice. (n.d.). About. Asian Americans Advancing Justice. Retrieved December 4, 2022, from https://www.advancingjustice-aajc.org/about

Balintec, V. (2022, April 3). Asians 'tired,' 'frustrated' as study shows hate is on the rise in Canada | CBC News. CBCnews. Retrieved December 4, 2022, from https://www.cbc.ca/news/canada/toronto/2-years-into-the-pandemic-anti-asian-hate-is-still-on-the-rise-in-canada-report-shows-1.6404034

Chavez, N., & Chen, N. (2022, March 16). Assaulted. harassed. This is the reality for Asian Americans a year after the Atlanta spa shootings. CNN. Retrieved November 20, 2022, from https://www.cnn.com/2022/03/16/us/atlanta-spa-shootings-anniversary

Gover, A. R., Harper, S. B., & Langton, L. (2020). Anti-Asian Hate Crime During the COVID-19 Pandemic: Exploring the Reproduction of Inequality. American journal of criminal justice : AJCJ, 45(4), 647–667. https://doi.org/10.1007/s12103-020-09545-1

Graham, R. (2021, March 17). 8 dead in Atlanta spa shootings, with fears of Anti-Asian bias. The New York Times. Retrieved November 21, 2022, from https://www.nytimes.com/live/2021/03/17/us/shooting-atlanta-acworth

Government of Canada. (2022, August 25). Disproportionate harm: Hate crime in Canada. Government of Canada. Retrieved November 29, 2022, from https://www.justice.gc.ca/eng/rp-pr/csj-sjc/crime/wd95_11-dt95_11/p2.html

Hong, N., & Bromwich, J. E. (2021, March 18). Asian-Americans are being attacked. why are hate crime charges so rare? The New York Times. Retrieved December 4, 2022, from https://www.nytimes.com/2021/03/18/nyregion/asian-hate-crimes.html

Ramachandran, V. (2021, March 18). What you can do to fight violence and racism against Asian Americans. PBS. Retrieved December 4, 2022, from https://www.pbs.org/newshour/nation/what-you-can-do-to-fight-violence-and-racism-against-asian-americans

Sharma, S. (2021, August 9). Pandemics: A history of discrimination. HealthMatch. Retrieved November 19, 2022, from https://healthmatch.io/blog/pandemics-a-history-of-discrimination

Stop AAPI Hate. (2021, June 17). Retrieved November 20, 2022, from https://stopaapihate.org/

Vera, A., & Reilly, L. (2022, March 1). Asian woman attacked last year in New York by man with rock has died, family says. CNN. Retrieved November 20, 2022, from https://edition.cnn.com/2022/02/28/us/guiying-ma-death-new-york-asian-hate-crime/index.html

Chapter 10
The Physical Health Effects of the COVID-19 Pandemic

By Paige Breedon

Introduction

The COVID-19 pandemic has caused immense consequences for individuals financially, mentally, and physically as well as countries' productivity and economies. Many direct and indirect repercussions have ensued and continue to be relevant as the looming endemic nature of the virus follows. Admittedly, being infected by the virus has a whole set of physical and mental effects that can impact one's ability to participate actively and contribute to society. Also, the topic of "long covid" has been of particular interest as this newly coined term refers to COVID-19 symptoms that linger in infected individuals ("Covid-19," 2022). Aside from the direct effects of COVID-19, the restrictions and measures adopted to combat the virus have also led to many indirect physical and mental health repercussions. Such efforts include limited access to sports and recreational services and programs and increased sedentarism, leading to decreased exercise and the adoption of poor eating habits (Ammar et al., 2020). Specifically, the following chapter intends to explore studies demonstrating how COVID-19 has impacted individuals' physical health both directly and indirectly. Also, how COVID-19 has led to the adoption of sedentary and unhealthy habits; lastly, the chapter will propose potential solutions to reduce the negative impact of the COVID-19 pandemic.

Firstly, it is essential to recognize the restrictions and policies adopted to limit the spread of the COVID-19 virus and their corresponding repercussions for individuals' health (Furtado et al., 2021). Examples of public health measures that some countries have implemented include closing gyms, schools, workplaces, and canceling organized sports and fitness programming, enforcing curfews, and social distancing protocols (Wilke et al., 2022). Although such measures are proposed and implemented with the best intentions to minimize the spread of the virus and keep individuals healthy and protected, they have unavoidable repercussions associated with them. Such repercussions include limiting individuals' social and physical activity and consequently negatively impacting people's mental and physical health.

Direct Physical Health Effects of COVID-19

Notable physical health repercussions of COVID-19 include symptoms such as fever or chills, cough, shortness of breath or difficulty breathing, fatigue, muscle or body aches, headache, loss of taste or smell, sore throat, congestion or runny nose, nausea or vomiting, and diarrhea ("Covid-19," 2022). In more extreme cases, being infected with COVID-19 can lead to being hospitalized, needing intensive care, requiring a ventilator to breathe, or even death ("Covid-19," 2022). It is also important to recognize certain factors that put individuals at greater risk for experiencing more severe effects of COVID-19. Such factors include being an older adult with underlying medical conditions such as cancer, chronic kidney or liver or lung disease, cystic fibrosis, dementia, diabetes, or a heart condition ("People with," n.d.). Also, being immune compromised or HIV positive, overweight or pregnant can also make one more susceptible to more extreme effects of COVID-19 ("People with," n.d.). Thus, the physical health effects can be much more extreme and even life-threatening for people in these higher-risk groups.

Post-COVID-19 syndrome is characterized by common symptoms such as fatigue, fever, difficulty breathing and cough ("Symptoms of," n.d.). Also other symptoms include neurological problems or mental health conditions, joint or muscle pain, heart symptoms or conditions, problems with digestion, blood clots and changes in the menstrual cycle ("Symptoms of," n.d.). One of the proposed reasons COVID-19 symptoms may linger is organ damage affecting the heart, kidneys, skin and brain ("Symptoms of," n.d.). Inflammation and problems with the immune system can also happen ("Symptoms of," n.d.). These effects could lead to new conditions, further complicating the patient's health. Another explanation as to why 'long COVID' persists could be due to individuals with COVID-19 requiring intensive care and, thus, through those experiences, becoming extremely physically or mentally weak or developing post-traumatic stress disorder ("Covid-19," 2022). Overall, the possibility for lingering symptoms of COVID-19 demonstrate the importance of combating the virus, as long-term effects are at stake.

Indirect Physical Health Effects of the COVID-19 Pandemic

Indirectly, physical health repercussions revolve around those associated with being less active due to the cancellation of sports, recreational facilities services, and in-person learning and working (Wilke et al., 2022). By canceling such things, individuals are more prone to being sedentary, not leaving the house or keeping up with their exercise regimes. Also, by being socially isolated from their friends, teammates, and school and work colleagues and/or having fears and worries associated with the pandemic, individuals may reap many adverse mental health effects that further perpetuate their cycle of sedentarism. Through such confinements, individuals may find themselves trapped in a cycle where they are less physically and socially active and are experiencing disturbed sleeping and eating habits, all of which can contribute to severe long-term repercussions for their health and well-being.

For instance, a study conducted by Ammar and colleagues (2020) surveyed 1047 participants from North Africa, Western Asia, Europe, and various countries and collected data on their vigorous-intensity activity, moderate-intensity activity, walking, total physical activity, time spent sitting, and dietary behaviors before and after confinement periods due to the COVID-19 pandemic. The study found that the number of days/weeks and minutes/day of vigorous-intensity physical activity compared to before home confinement decreased by 22.7% and 33.1%, respectively (Ammar et al., 2020). The moderate-intensity activity followed a similar trend, with a

24% decrease in days/weeks of moderate intensity during home confinement and a 33.4% decrease in the number of minutes/day (Ammar et al., 2020). Walking decreased by 35% days/week and 34% minutes/day (Ammar et al., 2020). The number of hours/day of sitting increased by 28.6% during home confinement (Ammar et al., 2020). Regarding food-related data, the percentage of responses indicating eating out of control either most of the time or always was higher, 20.4% for most of the time and 9.6% for always as opposed to 9.7% and 2.3%, respectively (Ammar et al., 2020). The study concluded that the survey results indicate a negative effect of home confinement as it has been associated with increased sedentary habits such as sitting and unhealthy eating behaviors (Ammar et al., 2020). The study emphasizes the immense physical health impact home confinement, a commonly adopted habit or enforced requirement of the COVID-19 pandemic, has had on individuals. Therefore, it is essential to consider these results when planning and enforcing protocols that restrict individuals and encourage home confinement.

Also, changes in workers' physical activity and sedentary behavior has been observed through the pandemic. A review conducted by Ráthonyi and colleagues (2021) involved literature searches focussing on the COVID-19 caused changes in physical activity and sedentary behavior among the adult working population. It was found in 76.4% of studies that a decrease in the amount of physical activity occurred during the COVID-19 pandemic (Ráthonyi et al., 2021). The review emphasizes the importance of staying active despite the circumstances, especially among the working population. As well, the study emphasizes the need for policies and public health bodies to work to motivate employees, especially those whose job is already quite sedentary (i.e. office workers) to be more active and propose interventions that can help to minimize the impacts of the COVID-19 pandemic on individuals physical health and behaviors (Ráthonyi et al., 2021).

Furthermore, the COVID-19 pandemic poses an ironic problem as it has caused immense stress in people's lives, such stress and anxiety that could help be alleviated by participation in sports or physical activity (McGuine et al., 2022). Unfortunately, such activities became extremely limited due to protocols and restrictions set in place to minimize the spread of the virus. Also, as previously mentioned, those at higher risk for COVID-19 are individuals who are overweight are more likely to be infected, hospitalized, and admitted to the ICU (Popkin et al., 2020), which can be linked to exercise regime and diet, which are negatively impacted by the social protocols of the pandemic (McGuine et al., 2022). Therefore, the longer the pandemic proceeds, the more individuals have the chance to develop into higher risk; thus, the cycle of havoc can proceed.

To illustrate, a cross-sectional study conducted by McGuine and colleagues (2022) aimed to identify the effect of playing a sport during the COVID-19 pandemic on student-athletes health and distributed an online survey in October 2020 to 559 Wisconsin high school athletes. A total of 388 stated they did not play an interscholastic sport at their school, whereas the remaining 257 did (McGuine et al., 2022). Of those who did, 148 attended schools that offered fall sports, with 69 attending in person (McGuine et al., 2022). The interscholastic sports athletes reported mental health scores that indicated little or no anxiety; in contrast, non-athletes were likelier to display scores indicating moderate to severe anxiety than the interscholastic athlete group (McGuine et al., 2022). Physical activity was 41% higher for the interscholastic sports group than the control group (McGuine et al., 2022).. The study demonstrates the drastic changes in physical and mental health observed after the cancellation of high school sports in the spring of 2022, thus emphasizing the importance of prioritizing mental and physical health, especially during such stressful times.

Additionally, a cross-sectional study conducted by Etajuri and colleagues (2022) administered an online questionnaire to 150 undergraduate dental students, of which 147 responded to questions asking about the student's demographic data, their concerns about academic achievement, and their opinion on their institutions' response, and the impact of the crisis on their mental and physical health. Most students expressed concerns about the pandemic's effect on their physical and emotional health, 85.8% and 76.9%, respectively (Etajuri et al., 2022). The study demonstrates how new procedures and norms due to the COVID-19 pandemic, i.e. online learning, can impact mental and physical health and reflects the need to consider these implications and minimize these adverse effects carefully.

Furthermore, it is important to acknowledge the especially immense physical and mental health effects the COVID-19 has caused children. Such health effects can include increased risk of obesity, diabetes, and cardiovascular disease as seen in a study conducted by Dunton and colleagues (2020). The study examined the effects of the COVID-19 pandemic on physical activity and sedentary behavior in U.S. children (Dunton et al., 2020). Measures included an assessment of physical activity and sedentary behavior of children on the previous day and perceived changes in levels of physical activity and sedentary behavior between pre-COVID (defined as February 2020) and early COVID-19 periods (defined as April to May of 2020) (Dunton, 2020). This assessment was completed by recruited parents of children. The results indicated that parents of older children (i.e. ages 9-13) versus younger children (i.e. ages 5-8) believed there was a greater decrease in their child's physical activity and increase in their sedentary behavior (Dunton et al., 2020). Also, children were more likely to complete physical activity at home or in their neighborhood during the early- versus the pre-COVID-19 periods (Dunton et al. 2020). Perhaps indicating a burnout or further decline in children's motivation or willingness to be active and participate in activities that keep them mentally and physically healthy. The repercussions of such findings can indicate that short-term changes in patterns of physical activity and sedentary behaviors can become more widely adopted and lead to increased obesity, diabetes, and cardiovascular disease in children (Dunton et al., 2020). The study ended by emphasizing the need for programmatic and policy strategies being geared towards promoting physical activity and reducing sedentary behaviors, and such programs and policies need to be implemented soon, especially given the decline in motivation and activity that has seen as the pandemic progresses (Dunton et al., 2020).

Although the focus of this chapter is on the physical health effects associated with COVID-19 infection or the corresponding pandemic, it is also important to acknowledge the mental health effects that have been observed as mental health and physical health are intimately connected. Also, if one is dealing with mental health issues due to the pandemic, that can then in turn influence their ability to be physically active and avoid sedentary behavior and thus mental health is an extremely relevant topic. Specifically, a study conducted by Fruehwirth and colleagues (2021) aimed to estimate the effect of the pandemic on the mental health of college students. It is important to acknowledge that college students and arguably students in general have been particularly vulnerable to the effects of the COVID-19 pandemic, as a shift has been observed towards online learning and less in person engagement. The study found that the prevalence of moderate-severe anxiety increased from 18.1% before the pandemic to 25.3% within four months after the pandemic began for the 419 first-year students aged 18 to 20 years at a large public university in North Carolina (Fruehwirth et al., 2021). The study reported that general difficulties associated with distance learning and social isolation were key contributors to the increase in both symptoms of anxiety and depression (Fruehwirth et al., 2021). The study proposed that colleges could play a role in reducing the impact COVID-19 has had on students' mental health by providing appropriate resources and making policies when possible that are less socially isolating (Fruehwirth et al., 2021).

Potential Solutions to Minimizing the Physical Health Impact of COVID-19

Overall, despite the need for increased public health procedures and restrictions to minimize the spread of the virus, immense physical and mental health repercussions have resulted due to limited access and cancellation of in-person activities and sports (Furtado et al., 2021). Such physical health repercussions can be seen for students, workers, and society. Therefore, it is important to be aware of these effects and implement only the necessary protocols to prevent diminishing returns. Potential solutions that should be considered as the COVID-19 pandemic comes to a close and for future occurrences of unexpected levels of a transmittable disease include providing alternative means of health programming, limiting complete closures, and/or increasing access to less risky sports and activities, i.e. ensuring outdoor facilities are available.

Solutions can include those targeted at the individual and thus requiring individuals to become accountable for their health by taking time to schedule physical activity and avoid sedentary habits as much as possible. For instance, individuals can follow along with online workout programs, implement a routine, and monitor their personal activity goals. Individuals can also reach out to friends and family online or if they are living with them and try to keep each other accountable. Many strategies exist and should be explored that can help individuals find new ways to be active despite the limitations of the COVID-19 pandemic. It should also be the duty of the physicians or health-care practitioners to be proactive in prescribing physician activities to patients during the COVID-19 pandemic (Pinto et al., 2020). This emphasis on the importance of physical activity made by healthcare professionals may help to encourage and remind individuals through the pandemic to prioritize their physician health.

Also, especially in the age of technology new applications can be developed to help keep individuals fit and accountable in prioritizing their physician health. For instance, a study conducted by Egan and colleagues (2021) aimed at co-designing and developing a novel mobile app to educate and support care workers in being physically active at home despite COVID-19 restrictions serves as a potential solution or means of helping individuals stay fit despite the unique circumstances of lockdowns and restrictions associated with COVID-19. The study found that integrating core physical activity guidelines into a co-designed smartphone app with functionality for users was feasible and promises to fill the gap of effective physician activity solutions for caregivers during the COVID-19 pandemic and going forward (Egan et al., 2021). It is innovations such as these that can be used to help combat the physical health toll that the COVID-19 pandemic has taken on individuals.

Alternatively, solutions can be targeted at larger populations and include providing resources, programs, and education to groups of people that will ultimately lead to the adoption of healthy habits and policies that reduce the physical health effects of the COVID-19 pandemic.

Conclusion

Overall, the COVID-19 pandemic has shown the world many immense physical consequences of being infected and obedient to new restrictions and protocols. The health repercussions include those initially associated with being infected and extend to individuals who are not necessarily directly infected but instead required to abide by health protocols and thus miss out on opportunities to participate in healthy habits and practices. Although these protocols are devised and implemented with the best intentions, much more must be done to promote better mental and physical health to keep protocols sustainable and prevent them from being counter-productive.

Although everyone has been affected by the COVID-19 pandemic in some capacity, some groups have been especially vulnerable due to policies being placed on them more specifically, such as children, athletes, students, and employees. Specifically, children can be seen as a vulnerable group to the wrath of the COVID-19 pandemic as seen in a study conducted by Dunton and colleagues (2020), as through the implementation of a variety of policies they have suffered immensely, i.e. losing access to sports and organized programming as well as in-person learning which has been linked to increased sedentary behaviors and decreased physical activity. As well, there appears to be a trend in the further decline of physical health as the COVID-19 pandemic has progressed which should also emphasize the need for immediate and sustainable action.

More generally anyone participating in sport programming could have missed out on such programming and opportunities to stay mentally and physically healthy due to restrictions put in place and workers have also faced new challenges to stay physically and mentally healthy and avoid sedentary behavior.

Considering the immense effects of the COVID-19 pandemic on society, productivity, and health it is of the utmost importance to consider ways in which existing policies can be modified or adapted to accommodate individuals best interests as well as keep in mind the dangers of contracting the virus. It is with great balance between making policies that accommodate public health and physical health that improvements can be seen in individuals' health and well-being. Additional solutions include providing resources and education to those on how to stay mentally and physically healthy and remain engaged in their school, work, and/or sport.

References

Ammar, A., Brach, M., Trabelsi, K., Chtourou, H., Boukhris, O., Masmoudi, L., … Simunic, B. (2020). Effects of COVID-19 Home Confinement on Eating Behaviour and Physical   Activity: Results of the ECLB-COVID19 International Online Survey. Nutrients, 12(6), 1583–. https://doi.org/10.3390/nu12061583

Covid-19: Long-term effects. (2022, June 28). Mayo Clinic. Retrieved November 20, 2022, from https://www.mayoclinic.org/diseases-conditions/coronavirus/in-depth/coronavirus-long-t rm-effects/art-20490351

Dunton, G. F., Do, B., & Wang, S. D. (2020). Early effects of the COVID-19 pandemic on physical activity and sedentary behavior in children living in the U.S. BMC Public Health, 20(1), 1351–1351. https://doi.org/10.1186/s12889-020-09429-3

Egan, K. J., Hodgson, W., Dunlop, M. D., Imperatore, G., Kirk, A., & Maguire, R. (2021). A Novel Mobile App ("CareFit") to Support Informal Caregivers to Undertake Regular Physical Activity From Home During and Beyond COVID-19 Restrictions: Co-design and Prototype Development Study. JMIR Formative Research, 5(10), e27358–e27358. https://doi.org/10.2196/27358

Etajuri, E. A., Mohd, N. R., Naimie, Z., & Ahmad, N. A. (2022). Undergraduate dental students' perspective of online learning and their physical and mental health during COVID-19 pandemic. PloS One, 17(6), e0270091–e0270091. https://doi.org/10.1371/journal.pone.0270091

Fruehwirth, J. C., Biswas, S., & Perreira, K. M. (2021). The Covid-19 pandemic and mental health of first-year college students: Examining the effect of Covid-19 stressors using longitudinal data. PloS One, 16(3), e0247999–e0247999. https://doi.org/10.1371/journal.pone.0247999

Furtado, G. E., Letieri, R. V., Caldo-Silva, A., Sardão, V. A., Teixeira, A. M., Barros, M. P., ...Bachi, A. L. L. (2021). Sustaining efficient immune functions with regular physical exercise in the COVID-19 era and beyond. European Journal of Clinical Investigation, 51(5), e13485–n/a. https://doi.org/10.1111/eci.13485

McGuine, T. A., M Biese, K., Hetzel, S. J., Schwarz, A., Kliethermes, S., Reardon, C. L., ...Watson, A. M. (2022). High School Sports During the COVID-19 Pandemic: The Effect of Sport Participation on the Health of Adolescents. Journal of Athletic Training, 57(1), 51–58. https://doi.org/10.4085/1062-6050-0121.21

People with certain medical conditions. (n.d.). Centers for Disease Control and Prevention. Retrieved November 20, 2022, from https://www.cdc.gov/coronavirus/2019-ncov/need-extra-precautions/people-with-medical-conditions.html

Pinto, A. J., Dunstan, D. W., Owen, N., Bonfá, E., & Gualano, B. (2020). Combating physical inactivity during the COVID-19 pandemic. Nature Reviews. Rheumatology, 16(7), 347–348. https://doi.org/10.1038/s41584-020-0427-z

O'Brien, T. (2021). Staying active during the pandemic. Research in Nursing & Health, 44(3), 418–419. https://doi.org/10.1002/nur.22125

Popkin, B. M., Du, S., Green, W. D., Beck, M. A., Algaith, T., Herbst, C. H., … Shekar, M. (2020). Individuals with obesity and COVID-19: A global perspective on the epidemiology and biological relationships. Obesity Reviews, 21(11), e13128–n/a. https://doi.org/10.1111/obr.13128

Ráthonyi, G., Kósa, K., Bács, Z., Ráthonyi-Ódor, K., Füzesi, I., Lengyel, P., & Bácsné Bába, É. (2021). Changes in Workers' Physical Activity and Sedentary Behavior during the COVID-19 Pandemic. Sustainability (Basel, Switzerland), 13(17), 9524–. https://doi.org/10.3390/su13179524

Symptoms of COVID-19. (n.d.). Centers for Disease Control and Prevention. Retrieved November 20, 2022, from https://www.cdc.gov/coronavirus/2019-ncov/symptoms-testing/symptoms.html

Wilke, J., Rahlf, A. L., Füzéki, E., Groneberg, D. A., Hespanhol, L., Mai, P., … Pillay, J. D. (2022). Physical Activity During Lockdowns Associated with the COVID-19 Pandemic: A Systematic Review and Multilevel Meta-analysis of 173 Studies with 320,636 Participants. Sports Medicine - Open, 8(1). https://doi.org/10.1186/s40798-022-00515-x

Chapter 11
Investigating the 1918 Spanish Flu pandemic and Understanding the Virus's pathogenicity.

By Kazma Faheem

The flu pandemic of 1918 killed 50 million to 100 million people around the globe (Johnson & Mueller, 2002; Taubenberger & Morens, 2006), and the H1N1 influenza virus was the culprit (Tumpey et al., 2005; CDC, n.d.). This paper investigates the virus's emergence, spread and pathology to better understand how the virus was successful in killing one-third of the world's population in 1918(Johnson & Mueller, 2002; Taubenberger & Morens, 2006). In order to move back in time to investigate the virus, one must grapple with the fundamentals of Influenza.

The Fundamentals of Influenza

Influenza is another term for flu, which is a virus that infects the host's respiratory system, such as the nose, throat, and lungs (Mayo Clinic Staff, 2022). Influenza and Cold are both viral infections; however, their patients have severe symptoms, such as extreme cough, headache, tiredness, fever, muscle ache, and appetite loss, which lasts up to ten days. In contrast, a Cold is less extreme and only affects the upper respiratory, causing runny nose, watery eyes, and throat irritation, and lasts a few days (IPAC Canada, n.d.). Influenza infects both animals and humans. Individuals who have: obesity, have chronic illnesses (such as heart, lung, kidney and asthma), weakened immune systems (due to cancer or an existing bacterial infection), are Native Americans or are pregnant can experience complications such: Pneumonia- air sacs fill with pus or liquid; Bronchitis-inflammation of lung airways; Asthma flare ups-causes shortness of breath; Heart illnesses; Ear infections, and

Acute Respiratory distress syndrome-fluid leaks into lungs (Mayo Clinic, n.d.; kidshealth, n.d.; Cleveland Clinic, n.d.; Hopkins, n.d.).

A, B, C and D are four types of influenza viruses; type A viruses not only cause seasonal flu infections but are the only viruses to cause a pandemic (CDC, n.d.). A pandemic refers to a contagious disease that infects countries around the globe at a higher rate, as can be seen when one looks at the Greek etymology of the word "Pan," meaning "all," and "demics" meaning "people" (Honigsbaum, 2009). However, not all Influenza A viruses are the same. Hemagglutinin (HA) and Neuraminidase (NA) are proteins on the virus's surfaces that appear as spikes on the virus, which help the virus attach and invade the host's cell, and scientists use HA and NA to categorize the types of Influenza A viruses (CDC, n.d.; Doucleff, 2013). Eighteen different kinds of Hemagglutinin and twelve different kinds of Neuraminidase appear on the viruses' surface; as a result, the type A viruses have 130 or more kinds of viruses, for example, H1N1, H4N6 (CDC, n.d.). Type A viruses can swap genetic information when two or more A viruses infect the host simultaneously, which makes Type A a cause for pandemics (CDC, n.d.). Furthermore, these viruses undergo major Antigenic shift, which refers to changes in the H and N proteins of the type A viruses that can result in a pandemic (IPAC Canada, n.d.)

To understand how the flu pandemic of 1918 ravaged countries around the globe, it is essential to understand the circumstances in which the virus began in the first place.

World War I: From Trenches to Immune System

More than sixty-five million civilians enlisted to fight in the Great World War I that began with the assassination of the Duke of Austria, which caused the British Empire and its Allies (including the United States) to declare War on Germany and its allies while countries like Spain remained neutral (HISTORY, n.d.; IWM, n.d.; Kruizinga, 2013). The War caused the deaths of more than sixteen million soldiers and civilians on both sides, of which an estimated twenty-one million people suffered wounds (HISTORY, n.d; Mougel, 2011). The figures do not include individuals affected by mental health disorders such as Post Traumatic Stress Disorder (PTSD) (HISTORY, n.d.).Symptoms included anxiety, tremors, and nightmares; it affected more than eighty thousand British soldiers alone; soldiers and civilians (even those who had not been near the battlefield) suffered (HISTORY, n.d.). Unsurprisingly, society at the time did not understand mental health disorders caused by the War, as German psychiatrists referred to men with PTSD as being "lazy, selfish and unpatriotic" (Lerner, 2000). However, research today has shown that PTSD in soldiers impairs the immune system and causes an array of autoimmune diseases: Multiple Sclerosis-the immune systems attacks nerves resulting in one's ability to walk, write, read or even talk; Systemic Lupus Erythematosus-the immune system attacks its tissues causing damage to organs such as lungs, and Rheumatoid Arthritis-immune system attacks body tissues which cause bone deterioration and joint disformity (Bookwalter et al., 2021; CDC, n.d., Hopkins, n.d., MAYOCLINIC, n.d., 2021). Also, during World War I, armies and civilians suffered from malnutrition and famine (Encyclopedia, 2021). More often, the armies targeted the food supply of the opposing army or the country, which resulted in civilians and armies being unable to feed themselves(Encyclopedia, 2021). This finding suggests that the effects of World War I were devastating to the immune systems of soldiers who became vulnerable to diseases such as Trench Foot-soldiers stood for long hours in wet Trenches, and as a result, their feet's skin would peel off and become infected by fungus, whose treatment was to apply whale oil or amputate the foot; Trench Fever-caused by the infected feces of the body louse in soldiers that would enter the lesions caused by the scratchings and result in muscle ache, fever followed by depression and there were no treatments other than bed rest, and finally, the Trench Mouth-when mouth dwelling bacteria overgrow, they caused gum bleeding and painful swelling caused by poor hygiene, stress and being in the trenches (Payne, 2008). For civilians, malnutrition and widespread food scarcity would have caused the immune systems to become vulnerable as well because research suggests that famine causes individuals to suffer from autoimmune diseases and disorders, which would prevent the body from having a functioning immune system (Harvard, n.d.). The finding demonstrates that PTSD, poor conditions in trenches and widespread famine around the globe caused a significantly weakened immune system that left soldiers and civilians vulnerable to catching various diseases, including the 1918 flu virus.

The Spanish Flu of 1918 did not begin in Spain; instead, the virus took its hold in Haskell County of Kansas, United States, with a population of roughly two thousand people in February 1918 (Barry, J. M., 2003). Dr. Loring Miner. Enamore worked as a physician and witnessed an unusual disease that not only did not discriminate between the ages of its victims but also caused its patients to develop Pneumonia, which resulted in the patient's death (Barry, J. M., 2003). Unfortunately, the news of the mysterious disease never made it to the local newspaper's front page due to the ongoing War (Barry, J. M., 2003). However, Dr. Miner wrote his findings in the Public Health Reports to warn public health officials about the mysterious disease that affected the people of Haskell who raised cattle and grains, resulted in illnesses and deaths and quickly disappeared (Barry, J. M., 2003). The journal published Dr. Miner's report in late March; by then, Army Camps in the US and other countries had already started to experience outbreaks. For example, in March of 1918, five hundred soldiers fell ill with the flu in Fort Riley and other camps in the US(kansapedia, 2012. However, no official visited the camp to investigate the illness because the soldiers suffered similar symptoms to those of Dr. Miner's patients; some died while others had a mild infection and, as a result, were sent to Europe (kansapedia, 2012). Dr.Miner's dire warning about the virus was published late in the journal. Due to outbreaks in other places, his warnings about the virus's potential to possibly be severe were neither taken seriously by countries nor heeded by public health officials. They became buried in the journal reporting death tolls and outbreaks(Barry, J. M., 2003). Therefore, the virus that hit Kansas county and Fort Riley with such force and evaporated in thin air had ample opportunity to adapt before it spread like wildfire.

The Virus Spreads

With the War needing more soldiers than ever, the soldiers were sent to Europe, which is the beginning of how the virus's first mild wave spread from the United States of America to other countries (Barry & J. M., 2003). The virus's first wave would have gone unnoticed if not for the Spanish King and the Prime Minister of Spain falling ill (Taubenberger et al., 2001). The newspapers in Spain started reporting, and because Spain was neutral then, the virus was called the "Spanish Flu" (Taubenberger et al., 2001). The first wave did cause deaths, but they were not high enough to sound off an alarm; additionally, countries were too busy with the War (Tsoucalas et al., 2016; Watanabe et al., 2011). The virus had enough time to adapt, and the mutations that occurred in the virus proved to be lethal in the fall and winter of 1918 (Tsoucalas et al., 2016; Watanabe et al., 2011). The trench conditions and the weakened immune system of the soldiers proved to be the perfect breeding ground for the 1918 flu virus. The virus began its two deadly waves, starting with soldiers who boarded ships with infected soldiers present or those who landed in other countries to join Allied forces, thus infecting the mode of transportation and any objects that came into their contact(Britannica, n.d.; Tsoucalas et al., 2016; Watanabe et al., 2011). On November 11th, 1918, World War I ended (Delaware.gov, n.d.). As soldiers began to return to their homes, the virus spilled to the civilian population (who also had weakened immune systems due to malnutrition and trauma). Soon the death rates went to the roof and the virus infected all age groups, especially pregnant women and individuals aged twenty to forty (Britannica, n.d.; Tsoucalas et al., 2016; Watanabe et al., 2011). However, an interesting feature of the virus was that though the Spanish flu infected all age groups, ninety-nine percent of deaths were in patients younger than 65 years old (Tsoucalas et al., 2016). This means that the population older than 65 had a better immune response to the virus than the younger population, which suggests that the old population had developed immunity to the virus due to the Russian flu pandemic of 1889 (Simonsen et al., 1998).

The virus infected the lung cells of the individual, which caused flu-like symptoms such as fever, cough, muscle pain and sore throat (Cleveland Clinic, n.d.). In addition, complications such as Pneumonia arose from the virus's infection, and death numbers rose due to the absence of antibiotics at the time (Watanabe et al., 2011).

Hospitals were flooded with wounded civilians and soldiers, and doctors were away serving in army camps, leaving medical school students and nurses to treat patients. Aspirin was one of the first medications administered to patients to numb pain because health professionals still thought the Spanish flu was just like any other flu (Rogers, 2020). However, Doctors and nurses administered Aspirin to infected patients in lethal amounts to cure the pain of coughing and muscle pain, which resulted in deaths due to the side effects of Aspirin, such as coma, convulsions, rapid breathing and brain swelling (Rogers, 2020; Watanabe et al., 2011). Moreover, desperate to try any method to cure the fatal flu, some observed that women who had traumatic miscarriages due to the virus or individuals who had bleeding of any sort or menstruated seemed to have beaten the Virus (Rogers, 2020; Greenstone, 2010). Hence, patients died due to 'bloodletting,' a 19th-century medical process that removed an excessive amount of the patient's blood to cure fever (Rogers, 2020; Greenstone, 2010).

Furthermore, some parents made their children inhale chlorine gas found in local gas works because many observed that the virus rarely infected those who worked with it. Although chlorine gas did kill pneumonia bacteria in infected children, it was also poisonous at the same time(Rogers, 2020). Unlike the other treatments, doctors tried experimental vaccines, which proved useless because no healthcare professional had the required knowledge about the Virus (Trilla, 2008). Adding to the woes of virus devastation was that Eastern countries, such as China and India, thought of the virus as an Evil spirit (Rogers, 2020). Therefore, it resulted in no isolation, quarantine or disinfection from infected individuals as family members tried to perform spirituals (Rogers, 2020).

On the other hand, countries did not apply health safety measures evenly at the beginning of the pandemic. For example, as countries began to experience the second and third waves of the virus, countries such as Spain banned spitting and disinfected streets, wagons, theaters, railways, and buildings (Moya, 2020; Rico-Avello, 1964; Trilla, 2008). Moreover, some countries implemented measures such as encouraging individuals to disinfect their noses and mouths with hydrogen peroxide or methanol and oil mixture (Moya, 2020; Rico-Avello, 1964; Trilla, 2008). Furthermore, countries enforced quarantine, curfews, banning large gatherings, maintaining healthy diets, resting, wearing masks and social distancing (Moya, 2020; Rico-Avello, 1964; Trilla, 2008).

The public health measures, though effective, did not prevent the virus from spreading, infecting and killing over 50 million to 100 million people around the globe until 1919, when those who contracted the virus gained immunity and the virus that once devastated countries soon disappeared (Amenabar, 2020; Britannica, n.d.; Johnson & Mueller, 2002; Taubenberger & Morens, 2006; Tsoucalas et al., 2016; Watanabe et al., 2011).

Understanding the Mysterious Virus

In order to understand the pathology of the Spanish flu of 1918, it was crucial to obtain the virus and determine what aspects of the virus enabled it to be contagious and multiply inside a host successfully (CDC). As a result, Ann Ried et al. published a paper in 1999 which constructed the flu's hemagglutinin (HA) genes (CDC, n.d.). The HA genes code for HA proteins on the virus's surface, which helps the virus infect the host's healthy lung cells (CDC, n.d.). The researchers gathered samples from three infected individuals who had all died from the virus in 1918 and successfully obtained the Spanish flu's RNA to determine the sequence of the HA gene in the Virus (CDC, n.d.; Ann Ried et al. al., 1999). The researchers found that the virus's ancestor infected humans between 1900 to 1915 (CDC, n.d.; Ann Ried et al., 1999).

Moreover, they also found that the virus originated in birds and, over time, infected swine and spilled into the human population(CDC, n.d.; Ann Ried et al., 1999). Furthermore, the researchers also noted that the HA gene had not gone through any genetic changes, which would result in its severity (CDC, n.d.; Ann Ried et al., 1999). Instead, the researchers concluded that there were perhaps different genetic changes within the virus, not just in one of its proteins, that enabled it to have a unique combination of RNA, resulting in widespread devastation (CDC, n.d.; Ann Ried et al., 1999). Several other researchers investigated which of the virus's eight genes made it virulent (CDC, n.d.). Each subsequent study focused on a different gene of the virus, such as NA genes and polymerase genes, and all reached the same conclusion as Ann Ried et al.; that the virulence of the virus was the result of eight unique genes (Ann Ried et al., 1999; Basler et al., 2001, CDC, n.d., Taubenberger et al., 2005). Finally, Dr. Tumpey recreated the virus in 2005 to understand its pathogenicity in a living host by gathering all the eight genes and plasmids of the virus and inserting them into a human kidney cell, which caused the cell to make the virus itself (CDC, n.d.). For several days Dr. Tumpey (who worked alone on constructing the virus and testing it on the living host) managed to get the lost virus to appear on the petri dish (CDC, n.d.). Following the reappearance of the ancient Virus, Dr. Tumpey decided to investigate the pathogenicity in mice and found that the virus was a hundred percent lethal. The virus could replicate itself in the infected at an unprecedented rate that caused mice to lose a considerable amount of their body weight and die within three days of the infection (CDC, n.d.; Tumpey et al., 2005).

Moreover, Dr. Tumpey found that the HA gene played a significant role in the severity of the Virus (CDC, n.d.; Tumpey et al., 2005). The doctor injected one group of mice with the virus itself and the other group with a combination of human Influenza and the remaining seven virus genes (CDC, n.d.; Tumpey et al., 2005). The researcher noted that mice with the virus died and lost body weight, while the other group did not die or suffer from weight loss (CDC, n.d.; Tumpey et al., 2005).

Furthermore, Dr. Tumpey found that the virus did not cause damage to vital organs, such heart, brain, liver and spleen, though the virus damaged the mice's lungs and human lung cells (CDC, n.d.; Tumpey et al., 2005). He noted that in mice, the infection caused lungs to fill up with fluid, their lung tissue to swell, and Pneumonia, similar to the victims of the 1918 Spanish flu (CDC, n.d.; Tumpey et al., 2005). In order to witness a glimpse into the virus's effects on the human lungs, the doctor infected one group of human lung cells with the virus. In contrast, the other group of human lung cells with a combination of the virus and the recent flu virus (CDC, n.d.; Tumpey et al., 2005). He measured the infections of both groups after twelve, sixteen and twenty-four hours(CDC, n.d.; Tumpey et al., 2005). The virus spread in the human lung cells fifty percent higher than the recombinant virus, which demonstrated that along with the HA gene, the polymerase gene (responsible for replicating and transcribing the viral genome) also contributed to the severity and virulence of the disease in humans (CDC, n.d.; Diffen, n.d.; Tumpey et al., 2005). To investigate whether the flu was H1N1 bird flu in nature or H1N1 mammalian flu, Dr. Tumpey infected a group of chicken egg embryos with the virus, some eggs with some genes of the virus while others with the H1N1 mammalian Virus (CDC, n.d.; Diffen, n.d.; Tumpey et al., 2005). The investigation saw that the virus was lethal to all chicken eggs, consistent with the earlier studies that bird flu is lethal to eggs (CDC, n.d.; Diffen, n.d.; Tumpey et al., 2005). The other group of eggs survived, which pointed to the conclusion that though HA and polymerase genes do have a significant role in the infectiousness of the virus, the virus itself has unique genes, which make it lethal to its living host and an Avian virus of origin (Ann Ried et al., 1999; Basler et al., 2001, CDC, n.d.,; Taubenberger et al., 2005; Tumpey et al., 2005).

Although the 1918 flu pandemic caused devastation in countries around the globe, the virus spread successfully because of the global World War that prioritized a political spat over millions of innocent soldiers' and civilians' health at risk. The War and the countries involved in it were simply pawns in the long game in which each side inflicted their species with PTSD, malnutrition, famine, and horrendous trench conditions that made the immune system vulnerable and powerless to different diseases and infections. With the War about to end, the virus spread because countries did not take it seriously, and people were immune-compromised. Moreover, the virus was also able to inflict and kill its victims due to the presence of superstitious and medieval Medical practices, which may have forced healthcare professionals to ponder on the absence of research and treatments on the virus. It would not be until the end of the 20th century and the dawn of the 21st century that researchers unearthed the virus and witnessed the pathogenicity of the virus in the living host. Though one can argue that since the virus was lethal in mice and human lung cells, it was lethal to humans, to begin with, whether the War resulted in individuals' weakened immune systems is an irrelevant argument. The argument is valid; however, it fails to consider that the virus caused deaths in the young population (who were avid participants in the War, by the way) as opposed to the older population (aged 65 and older) because they already had antibodies due to infection from the Russian pandemic. The virus's lethality and infectiousness are a stark reminder of how countries' ignorance during 1918 cost millions of innocent lives. If countries had ended the War and put their differences aside, the health safety measures could have been applied evenly to all countries around the globe. Thus, resources to fight the War could have been allocated to discovering a treatment.

References

Amenabar. (2020). 'The 1918 flu is still with us': The deadliest pandemic ever is still causing problems today. The Washington Post. https://www.washingtonpost.com/history/2020/09/01/1918-flu-pandemic-end/

Asthma Flare-Ups (for Parents) - Nemours KidsHealth. (n.d.). https://kidshealth.org/en/parents/flare-up.html

Avello. (1964). La epidemia de gripe: 1918-1919. Gaceta Médica Española, 38(1–4).

Barry, J. M. (2004). The site of origin of the 1918 influenza pandemic and its public health implications. Journal of Translational Medicine, 2(1), 3. https://doi.org/10.1186/1479-5876-2-3

Basler, C. F., Reid, A. H., Dybing, J. K., Janczewski, T. A., Fanning, T. G., Zheng, H., Salvatore, M., Perdue, M. L., Swayne, D. E., García-Sastre, A., Palese, P., & Taubenberger, J. K. (2001). Sequence of the 1918 pandemic influenza virus nonstructural gene (NS) segment and characterization of recombinant viruses bearing the 1918 NS genes. Proceedings of the National Academy of Sciences, 98(5), 2746–2751. https://doi.org/10.1073/pnas.031575198

Betrán Moya, & José Luis. (2005). Historia de las epidemias en España y sus colonias (1348-1919). La Esfera De Los Libros, 1348–1919. Blakemore, E. (2019, June 21). When Germany Called its Soldiers Hysterical. JSTOR Daily. https://daily.jstor.org/when-germany-called-its-soldiers-hysterical/

Bookwalter, D. B. (2020, January 15). Posttraumatic stress disorder and risk of selected autoimmune diseases among US military personnel - BMC Psychiatry. BioMed Central. https://bmcpsychiatry.biomedcentral.com/articles/10.1186/s12888-020-2432-9

Bronchitis: Causes, Symptoms, Diagnosis & Treatment. (n.d.). Cleveland Clinic. https://my.clevelandclinic.org/health/diseases/3993-bronchitis

Doucleff, M. (2013, May 7). What's In A Flu Name? H's And N's Tell A Tale. NPR.org. https://www.npr.org/sections/health-shots/2013/05/07/180808276/whats-in-a-flu-name-hs-and-ns-tell-a-tale

Flu Pandemic of 1918 - Kansapedia - Kansas Historical Society. (n.d.-a). https://www.kshs.org/kansapedia/flu-pandemic-of-1918/17805

Flu Pandemic of 1918 - Kansapedia - Kansas Historical Society. (n.d.-b). https://www.kshs.org/kansapedia/flu-pandemic-of-1918/17805

Food and Nutrition | International Encyclopedia of the First World War (WW1). (n.d.). https://encyclopedia.1914-1918-online.net/article/food_and_nutrition

History.com Editors. (2018, August 21). PTSD and Shell Shock. HISTORY. https://www.history.com/topics/inventions/history-of-ptsd-and-shell-shock

History.com Editors. (2022, August 9). World War I. HISTORY. https://www.history.com/topics/world-war-i/world-war-i-history

Honigsbaum, M. (2009, June 6). Pandemic. The Lancet. https://www.thelancet.com/journals/lancet/article/PIIS0140673609610539/fulltext

Imperial War Museums. (n.d.-a). 5 Things You Need To Know About The First World War. https://www.iwm.org.uk/history/5-things-you-need-to-know-about-the-first-world-war

Imperial War Museums. (n.d.-b). 5 Things You Need To Know About The First World War. https://www.iwm.org.uk/history/5-things-you-need-to-know-about-the-first-world-war

Influenza | Definition, Symptoms, Treatment, & Prevention. (1998, July 20). Encyclopedia Britannica. https://www.britannica.com/science/influenza/Influenza-pandemic-preparedness

Influenza Resources | IPAC Canada. (n.d.). https://ipac-canada.org/influenza-resources

JOHNSON, & MUELLER. (2002). Global Mortality of the 1918-1920 "Spanish" Influenza Pandemic. Bulletin of the History of Medicine. JSTOR. Retrieved December 3, 2022, from https://www.jstor.org/stable/44446153

Kruizinga, S. (n.d.). Neutrality (Chapter 20) - The Cambridge History of the First World War. Cambridge Core. https://www.cambridge.org/core/books/abs/cambridge-history-of-the-first-world-war/neutrality/8E25380E012F03851862070F7B34D46F

Mayo Clinic Staff. (2022, October 15). Influenza (flu) - Symptoms and causes. Mayo Clinic. https://www.mayoclinic.org/diseases-conditions/flu/symptoms-causes/syc-20351719

McNamara, L. (2015, October 6). What is Multiple Sclerosis (MS)? | The Johns Hopkins Multiple Sclerosis Center. https://www.hopkinsmedicine.org/neurology_neurosurgery/centers_clinics/multiple_sclerosis/conditions/

Morens, D., & Fauci, A. (2007). The 1918 Influenza Pandemic: Insights for the 21st Century. The Journal of Infectious Diseases, 195(7), 1018–1028. https://doi.org/10.1086/511989

Mougel. (2011). World War I casualties. REPERES. http://www.centre-robert-schuman.org/?page=404 Nutrition and Immunity. (2021, January 27). The Nutrition Source. https://www.hsph.harvard.edu/nutritionsource/nutrition-and-immunity/

Pneumonia. (n.d.). Johns Hopkins Medicine. https://www.hopkinsmedicine.org/health/conditions-and-diseases/pneumonia

Reid, A. H., Fanning, T. G., Hultin, J. V., & Taubenberger, J. K. (1999). Origin and evolution of the 1918 "Spanish" influenza virus hemagglutinin gene. Proceedings of the National Academy of Sciences, 96(4), 1651–1656. https://doi.org/10.1073/pnas.96.4.1651

Replication vs Transcription. (n.d.). Diffen. https://www.diffen.com/difference/Replication_vs_Transcription

Rheumatoid arthritis - Symptoms and causes. (2021, May 18). Mayo Clinic. https://www.mayoclinic.org/diseases-conditions/rheumatoid-arthritis/symptoms-causes/syc-20353648

Simonsen, L., Clarke, M. J., Schonberger, L. B., Arden, N. H., Cox, N. J., & Fukuda, K. (1998). Pandemic versus Epidemic Influenza Mortality: A Pattern of Changing Age Distribution. Journal of Infectious Diseases, 178(1), 53–60. https://doi.org/10.1086/515616

Systemic lupuserythematosus (SLE). (2022, July 5). Centers for Disease Control and Prevention. https://www.cdc.gov/lupus/facts/detailed.html

Taubenberger, J. K. (n.d.). 1918 Influenza: the Mother of All Pandemics. Emerging Infectious Diseases Journal. https://wwwnc.cdc.gov/eid/article/12/1/05-0979_article

Taubenberger, J. K., Reid, A. H., Janczewski, T. A., & Fanning, T. G. (2001). Integrating historical, clinical and molecular genetic data in order to explain the origin and virulence of the 1918 Spanish influenza virus. Philosophical Transactions of the Royal Society of London. Series B: Biological Sciences, 356(1416), 1829–1839. https://doi.org/10.1098/rstb.2001.1020

Taubenberger, J. K., Reid, A. H., Krafft, A. E., Bijwaard, K. E., & Fanning, T. G. (1997). Initial Genetic Characterization of the 1918 "Spanish" Influenza Virus. Science, 275(5307), 1793–1796. https://doi.org/10.1126/science.275.5307.1793

Taubenberger, J. K., Reid, A. H., Lourens, R. M., Wang, R., Jin, G., & Fanning, T. G. (2005). Characterization of the 1918 influenza virus polymerase genes. Nature, 437(7060), 889–893. https://doi.org/10.1038/nature04230

The Editors of Encyclopaedia Britannica. (1998, July 20). Influenza Pandemic Of 1918–19 | Cause, Origin, & Spread. Encyclopedia Britannica. https://www.britannica.com/event/influenza-pandemic-of-1918-1919

The Great War Ends. (2021, April 20). Division of Historical and Cultural Affairs - State of Delaware. https://history.delaware.gov/world-war-i/conclusion-ww1/

Trench Diseases of the First World War | The Western Front Association. (n.d.-a). https://www.westernfrontassociation.com/world-war-i-articles/trench-diseases-of-the-first-world-war/

Trench Diseases of the First World War | The Western Front Association. (n.d.-b). https://www.westernfrontassociation.com/world-war-i-articles/trench-diseases-of-the-first-world-war/

Trilla, A., Trilla, G., & Daer, C. (2008). The 1918 "Spanish Flu" in Spain. Clinical Infectious Diseases, 47(5), 668–673. https://doi.org/10.1086/590567

Tsoucalas, G. (2016, October 28). The 1918 Spanish Flu Pandemic, the Origins of the H1N1-virus Strain, a Glance in History :: Science Publishing Group. http://article.ejcbs.org/html/10.11648.j.ejcbs.20160204.11.html

Tumpey, T. M., Basler, C. F., Aguilar, P. V., Zeng, H., Solórzano, A., Swayne, D. E., Cox, N. J.,

Katz, J. M., Taubenberger, J. K., Palese, P., & García-Sastre, A. (2005). Characterization of the Reconstructed 1918 Spanish Influenza Pandemic Virus. Science, 310(5745), 77–80. https://doi.org/10.1126/science.1119392

Types of Influenza Viruses. (2022, December 2). Centers for Disease Control and Prevention. https://www.cdc.gov/flu/about/viruses/types.htm

Conclusion

The complexity of global pandemics are many folds; it requires in-depth analysis on root problems, sources for overlapping issues, and potential next steps to alleviate the uncovered effects. By recognizing and learning more from every pandemic, global development will enable greater anticipation & defensive steps to be taken. Such measures will continue advancing to minimize setbacks while pushing humanity towards a brighter future.

www.ingramcontent.com/pod-product-compliance
Lightning Source LLC
Chambersburg PA
CBHW030852270326
41928CB00008B/1331